جائزة الشيخ زايد للكتاب
Sheikh Zayed Book Award

Celebrating the very best writing from across the Arab world

The Sheikh Zayed Book Awards are one of the world's most ambitious and lucrative sets of awards, showcasing pre-eminent Arabic works and recognising leading figures in Arabic culture in a range of award categories.

Recognising Creativity تقدير لكل مبدع

2020 Sheikh Zayed Book Award Winners

Find out more about the Sheikh Zayed Book Award winners at: www.zayedaward.ae

GRANTA

12 Addison Avenue, London W11 4QR | email: editorial@granta.com
To subscribe go to granta.com, or call 020 8955 7011 in the United Kingdom, 845-267-3031
(toll-free 866-438-6150) in the United States

ISSUE 152: SUMMER 2020

PUBLISHER AND EDITOR	Sigrid Rausing
DEPUTY EDITOR	Rosalind Porter
POETRY EDITOR	Rachael Allen
DIGITAL DIRECTOR	Luke Neima
MANAGING EDITOR	Eleanor Chandler
SENIOR DESIGNER	Daniela Silva
ASSISTANT EDITOR	Josie Mitchell
EDITORIAL ASSISTANT	Lucy Diver
COMMERCIAL DIRECTOR	Noel Murphy
OPERATIONS AND SUBSCRIPTIONS	Mercedes Forest
MARKETING	Aubrie Artiano, Simon Heafield
PUBLICITY	Pru Rowlandson, publicity@granta.com
CONTRACTS	Isabella Depiazzi
TO ADVERTISE CONTACT	Renata Molina Lopes
	Renata.Molina-Lopes@granta.com
FINANCE	Mercedes Forest, Sofia Themistocli,
	Elizabeth Wedmore
SALES MANAGER	Katie Hayward
IT SUPPORT	Kieran Spiers, Mark Williams
PRODUCTION ASSOCIATE	Sarah Wasley
PROOFS	Katherine Fry, Jessica Kelly, Lesley Levene,
	Jess Porter
CONTRIBUTING EDITORS	Anne Carson, Mohsin Hamid, Isabel Hilton,
	Michael Hofmann, A.M. Homes, Janet Malcolm,
	Adam Nicolson, Leanne Shapton, Edmund White

THE WORLD TODAY

CHATHAM HOUSE'S INTERNATIONAL AFFAIRS MAGAZINE

SIX EDITIONS A YEAR | EXCLUSIVE ONLINE CONTENT INCLUDING
A SEARCHABLE ARCHIVE OF THE PAST 20 YEARS | WEEKLY INSIGHTS
INTO WORLD AFFAIRS | SUBSCRIPTIONS FROM £32

To subscribe go to www.theworldtoday.org. For any enquiries relating to marketing and
subscriptions, please contact Roxana Raileanu by email: RRaileanu@chathamhouse.org

eye

THE INTERNATIONAL REVIEW OF GRAPHIC DESIGN 100

Talking about graphic design

Eye is the world's most beautiful and collectable graphic design journal, packed with informed writing about design, photography, typography, illustration and more. Eye 100 is an unmissable special issue, essential for anyone interested in visual culture. Buy or subscribe
eyemagazine.com

CONTENTS

Introduction

What week of lockdown are we in, as I write this? I hardly know any more. Quite early on, walking at dusk, I heard whooping and clapping from houses far away, the sound carried on the wind. I stood in a field thinking of all the people who have died, and the dedication of those who had cared for them.

But soon everything that had felt so tragic and dramatic to begin with – thousands of people ill and dying, the great pause, the intense dreams, the solidarity clapping – came to feel normal. Lethargy took over, until that too wore away. I suppose most of us got used to our restricted worlds, moods and thoughts blooming and fading, and the almost imperceptible succession of phases, to do with how the light falls into a room, say, or how a new particular thing – a book, a film, a habit – establishes itself.

In Britain, a question is taken from a member of the public in the daily political briefings. A hushed voice reminds us that the Cabinet member present *has not seen the question in advance*, as though this were a political satire or a rehearsal, a performance of national tragedy rather than the real thing.

Alone, we stare moodily at our screens, then join meetings and smile with relief when people we know look back, face to face.

'What have we learned from the pieces coming in during this time?' I asked at an editorial meeting.

'Maybe,' someone answered, 'that many of us already had a fragile connection with the outside world.' It must be partly the nature of writing life, but the pieces in this issue all, in some way or other, speak to confinement or escape. Emma Cline's story is set in a closed center, 'not quite rehab but some way station before rehab'. The inmates include a famous TV chef: 'Thora had read every disgusting thing G. had done'; 'every hot-tub dickgraze' and 'drugged-up gropes of cowering PAs in sensible flats'. Thora herself had created teen avatars for her own gratification, not the only reason she is here. The atmosphere, or rather Thora's state of mind, is dense with cynicism, seduction and loneliness; too dense and complex, one senses, for the nature of the care (vitamins and counselling). Ann Beattie's protagonist opens a literary magazine and is shocked to see a photograph of her younger self with a friend and their college professor, illustrating a piece written by her former friend, an essay masquerading as fiction, inventing a love triangle in cadences that – adding insult to injury – seem an imitation of her own way of speaking when younger. Adam Nicolson's story of a seventeenth-century English village struck by the plague reminds us how close we are to that world still, forming theories from rumours and portents, fleeing, drinking, burying the dead.

But we are also learning to pay attention. To properly see. Here is Leanne Shapton, painting interior scenes from her flat in New York, and describing what she sees. Here is Teju Cole, observing trees from walks in Cambridge, Massachusetts, and Michael Hofmann, noticing 'drifts of pollen in the gutters and on car windscreens, like gold dust', in Gainesville, Florida.

Time is the gift, but of course there are bigger issues to grapple with; questions of freedom and captivity, of responsibility and existential threat. I could go on, finding words for dysfunctional or ineffective governance. If I don't, it's not from lack of interest, exactly – but the spittle of the spittlebugs on a thousand stalks of grass this morning seems more real to me now; or the hornet searching every corner of my room before it leaves, duty done. The light filters through the leaves outside my window; something moves – a dragonfly? No, a spiderweb, swaying in the wind.

I am not talking about beauty. Barry Lopez has described how observing a scene (a bear, say, feeding from a carcass) without automatically collapsing the moment into language, deepens the experience of seeing. His message applies to this pandemic too. I hope that by the time you read this, the lockdown will be over. Until then, I will be mindful of Lopez's rules: 'Perhaps the first rule of everything we endeavor to do is to pay attention. Perhaps the second is to be patient. And perhaps a third is to be attentive to what the body knows.' ∎

Sigrid Rausing

© ELISABETH McBRIEN
California Afternoon, 2017
New York Academy of Art

A/S/L

Emma Cline

Mountain, mountain, mountain. Mountains on every side. Mountains that looked pixelated by gravel and chaparral, mountains that looked like their faces were crumbling. At certain hours of the day, with the sun disappeared and the mountains outlined, the mountain range looked like a tidal wave, about to crash down, about to sweep everything clean.

The steady desert heat meant Thora applied and reapplied medicated lip balm, refilled her water bottle from communal jugs, water tinted by lemon slices and mint. They weren't allowed cell phones but could call home as much as they liked – after the first week, anyway. They could go into town with staff supervision. Thora didn't leave the Center, but her roommate, Ally, came back with turquoise dreamcatchers and magazines, big Saran-Wrapped cookies from the bakery.

When Thora wasn't in group, or doing check-ins with her counselor, she and Ally sat out by the pool in terry cloth robes, on lounge chairs that smelled a little moldy. Ally was twenty, the daughter of a senator. She wondered aloud how many Instagram followers she might have lost over the last month without her phone. Because Ally had diabetes, the staff let her keep her insulin and syringes, which she carried around in a pink zip-purse with a crown on it.

KEEP CALM AND CARRY ON.

Thora liked to watch Ally inject herself, pooch up the pale skin above her waistband. It was almost like doing drugs herself.

All in all, it was a nice place. The landscaping was professional, attended to by many sunburned men. The food had a pre-chewed quality, lots of purees and smoothies, though, famously, the meals were good, better than at other places. Thora could attest to that, no soggy chicken fingers, no frozen chocolate cake crispy with ice shards. They were well nourished. The staff gave out vitamins in plastic organizers, grainy vitamins, probiotics in gummy form, which was another way to tell this was not quite rehab but some way station before rehab, the rules loosely enforced, the idea of authority introduced without the necessary follow-through.

It was more of a holding pen, a quiet place – it was assumed that everyone there was very tired. They were all overworked, stressed, and perhaps that had led them to make bad decisions that had adversely affected the people around them. The Media Room was stacked with old Academy screeners, though every night for the last two weeks, Ally and Thora had watched a Ken Burns documentary about national parks. This alone seemed to take years off their lives.

When Thora called James, once a day, she could tell he was summoning a sort of gravitas, performing a solemnity he would later report to his therapist. He was attempting, she realized, to be present. Thora had only been gone two weeks: already James had started to seem theoretical, a series of still photos that didn't quite coalesce into someone she had married.

'You sound strong,' James said. 'Really.'

'Mm,' Thora said.

'I love you,' James said, somber, his voice dropping an octave.

For a moment, she studied the silence between them with curiosity: suddenly she could do things like this, stop answering, stop talking, and it was fine.

She forced herself to speak. 'I love you, too.' James was, she knew, not a bad person.

They were bored, lights out, Thora's headlamp illuminating the corners of the room: the not-bad abstract paintings, the window cracked to let in the chilly night air. Outside were the dark shapes of the big aloe plants, the cacti. Thora stared at the twin beds, the matching coverlets. She hadn't shared a room since college. It had been so long ago: she couldn't remember if she'd actually liked any of her friends, the girl she lived with who kept her hair short, who baked loaves of sourdough in the dorm kitchen. She was a wilderness guide now. Thora was sure her life would seem appalling to the girl. Maybe it was.

Ally slept naked. Thora could've complained about this, she guessed – complaints were almost encouraged, showed they were setting limits and responding proactively to their environments – but she didn't care. Thora liked the blunt fact of Ally's presence, liked watching Ally move around, inspecting one of her pale tits for nipple hair under the lamplight. They took away Ally's tweezers after she plucked every hair from her left armpit, though she showed Thora she could do it with her fingernails, too. She often fell asleep with one hand on her crotch, as if it was a pet. That night, Ally was reading the book she'd been reading the last two weeks. Thora had seen a lot of people carrying the book around the Center: making a big deal of bringing it to lunch, women squeezing the hardcover tightly to their chests as they walked to Restorative Yoga.

'Can I see?' Thora said. Ally passed it over.

Thora read just a few pages. It was about a plucky doll maker in occupied Paris during World War II. It seemed like a book for people who hated books.

'This is terrible,' Thora said, flipping the book to see the author photo. A woman stared back from a razzle of Aztec jewelry. 'The author looks like the world's most cheerful nine-year-old.'

'It's actually really good,' Ally said, snatching it back. Thora had hurt her feelings.

'Sorry,' Thora said. Ally didn't respond, on the edge of pouting. She had pulled the covers up over herself, turning away from Thora.

'Wanna test my blood?' Thora said.

At this, Ally brightened. She sat up. She had been begging to test Thora's blood sugar.

'Come here,' she said, patting her bed, taking out her little pink purse. Suddenly she seemed very professional, despite her nudity.

Ally held Thora's right hand in hers, palm up, the fingers splayed. 'Here we go.'

She jabbed Thora's finger, then held a tissue to it to absorb the drop of red. It stung worse than she had imagined it might. Thora sucked her fingertip hard.

'You do this to yourself all the time?'

'One-oh-five,' Ally said, briskly, after feeding the paper slip into her little machine. 'Very nice.'

Ally dropped the used needle into an empty seltzer bottle, a poky mess of trash and bloody napkins that she kept on her nightstand, like a gory snow globe.

Thora woke in the blue morning light, Ally's voice coming from the bed next to her. 'The people are eating,' she muttered. 'The people are eating.' The medication Ally was taking seemed to make her a little crazy. When Thora went to check on her, she saw Ally was still asleep, a pillow clenched between her knees.

'You just kept repeating yourself,' Thora told her at breakfast. 'Over and over.'

Ally pushed for details, asking Thora whether she'd said anything else. 'I can handle it,' she said, 'just tell me,' and it struck Thora that Ally wasn't nervously patrolling the spill of her psyche, worried about what poisonous things she'd let slip, but that Ally genuinely hoped to learn something valuable and unknown about herself.

Before she'd come here, Thora had gotten in what her counselor Melanie would call a bad spiral.

It was the afternoons that did it, three o'clock like a kind of death knell, the house seeming too still, too many hours of sunlight left in the day. How had Thora even started going to the chat rooms? The last time she had been in a chat room was in high school, sleepovers where girls crowded around a desktop computer and wrote sickening things to men, all of it a joke, then furtively masturbated in their sleeping bags. Or at least Thora had. And now she was back, typing in a username.

Thora18.

How quickly the messages had come in:

Hey Thora! Cute name Asl

Asl

Wanna chat Asl?

Are you 18 or 18 isshhh

It amused her, on her laptop in bed, her husband at work, to reply to these men. To conjure an eighteen-year-old that did not exist, an eighteen-year-old that Thora had never been, certainly: blond, blue-eyed, a member of the cheerleading squad. Did high schools still have cheerleading squads? Had they ever? It didn't matter how ridiculous the things she said were, how big she made her tits, how short she made the skirt of her supposed cheer uniform, the men seemed to believe, wholeheartedly, that she was real. A ludicrous illusion they were building together, and she found she enjoyed the back and forth. Pretending not to know why the men were chatting with her. Writing *hahahaha* whenever they brought up sex. *What's that,* she typed when someone mentioned double penetration. When they asked her pointed, leading questions about her *real age,* she finally agreed that she was, in fact, only sixteen.

They were ecstatic, writing back instantly, the sudden use of exclamation points like cardiograms from their throbbing erections:

I won't tell babe don't worry!!!!

Her stupidity delighted these men. They had found her, at last: a teen cheerleader who wanted to learn about sex, who wanted to learn about it from them! Too stupid to understand what they were taking from her!

After a while they wanted photos. She ignored the requests, usually, closing the window, but then she thought, why not?

She spent a good hour on the bed, trying to take a photo with her face mostly hidden, a photo where she didn't look thirty-five but instead looked like a teenager: a finger in her mouth, her tongue peeping out like a little cat. Her tongue looked strange, too pale, but if she used a filter, one arm covering her nipples, she might look eighteen.

The men loved the photo. But then they wanted more.

Are you shaved?

Oh ya, she said. She was not.

How many dicks have you seen.

Um, she would type. *2. Is that weird?*

Have you ever had a boyfriend?

No, she typed. *I wisshhhhhh!*

Amazing how this ate up the afternoon, four hours passing without Thora looking up from the screen. She had missed two texts from James.

If she had better friends, she would have told them about what she was doing. Or if James was a different kind of person. Because wasn't it sort of funny? She had an entire run of photos of herself on her phone now: bending over, the seat of her underwear pulled tightly across her ass, pictures of her face from the nose down, a nipple between her fingers. They all wanted a pussy shot: she found one off the internet to use. She sent the same photo every time, so gradually she began to believe this bare pink pussy was her own pussy, and in fact began to feel proud of just how perfect this pussy – her pussy! – was.

She had never been the focus of so much attention. So many men trying to coax or trick her into giving them what they wanted. And that was the part she liked best, the knowing/unknowing – it wasn't possible to summon artificially, role play wouldn't do it. It had to be real.

She only hated them when they got mean: when she told them she had to go, and they typed back, furious.

Are u fucking serious just help me cum pls

Pls

Im so hard
Bitch

When Thora got bored of talking to the same men, she started signing in under different names. Usually under *James45*. Sometimes *DaddyXO*. She talked with the men, pretended she was a man, too, and they sent her photos of teens in bikinis at public pools and she sent them photos of herself.

Such a whore, she typed. *Little teen whore.*

Mmmm fuck, a man typed back. *Love those teen tits.*

It seemed obvious that the photos of her were not photos of a teenager, but no matter. Their wish that the tits belonged to a teenager was so strong that it created an alternate reality. She had never been so excited: seeing herself as these men did, some unformed idiot who needed to be fucked. Her sheets smelled like sweat, all the curtains drawn. She didn't eat for whole days.

'You're so wet,' James said one night, surprised, when she put his hand in her underwear. But then they had sex the way they always did, James coming on her stomach, his body jerking in a series of convulsions, as though he were being riddled with bullets at the O.K. Corral.

It had all seemed funny except that, truly, she would rather do this than anything else: run the usual errands that kept things in motion, see James, have dinner with him. It was like having a calling, finally, the way she had once imagined she might. A life organized around a higher goal. While James slept, his back turned to her and the covers kicked off, she typed furtively on her phone to men who sent photos of dicks, sometimes tiny squibs of flesh between massively fat thighs, sometimes overlarge penises with the porn watermark visible in the corner.

Wow, she always typed. *I don't know if it will fit.*

That was not the reason she had ended up at the Center, exactly, the chats, but it hadn't helped.

There was a hike in the morning, before the temperatures got unbearable. On the drive to the trailhead, Melanie had turned the radio to a Christian talk station Thora mistook for NPR until they said 'resurrection' one too many times.

Thora scrambled around the boulders, up through the dust and the sage. She drank lukewarm water; Melanie passed out protein bars. Last session, someone kept mashing these into coils and leaving them in the urinals, or so said Ally, a veteran of the program. It was a real problem, fake shit being essentially as difficult to clean as real shit. Was there a lesson there?

By the time they got back, G. had already arrived.

No one had known he was coming. He looked, if anything, exactly like the person in the newspaper photos – froggish, squashed, well fed. For all five seasons of his show, he had been clean-shaven, ruddy in his apron and concert T-shirts, big moony face damp with steam from whatever was cooking on the stove. Now he'd grown stubble, white, extending beyond his jawline to his neck and cheeks, giving his face the semblance of a shape. He wore a baseball hat and the same baggy clothes as the rest of them – sweatshirts, pants with soft waists. Their days were considered difficult enough that whatever energy they may have once expended on buttons and zippers was now worth diverting elsewhere.

Men and women were kept separate except for lunch, which most people ate in their rooms anyway. G., surprisingly, chose to eat at a shaded picnic table by the pool, close enough for Thora and Ally to study his froggy face for signs of evil, watch him pick at a sweet potato drowned in soy sauce. Did he eat the sweet potato in a particularly evil way?

The staff allowed them their benzos and SSRIs as long as their home doctors kept the prescriptions current. Things like this made it hard to believe that the people who worked there actually thought they were helping anyone. Ally and Thora sometimes swapped meds for fun; Thora took one dose of Ally's Lexapro and went into what felt like a light mania, pedaling the stationary bike for a solid hour, then eating ravenously, spilling salsa verde on her robe. The night that G.

arrived, Ally took someone's Ambien but stayed awake, filling out her Dialectic Behavioral Workbook.

What are three concrete changes you can make in order to improve your life?

She showed Thora her answers the next morning, written in loopy Ambien scrawl:

1. *Buy puffy white sneakers*
2. *Double pierce my ears*
3. *Fuck G.*

Addled as she'd been on a sedative-hypnotic, Ally brought up a good point: who was G. gonna fuck first?

G. was assigned Robert as his sober coach, tiny Robert who told everyone with pride that he had built the woodfired pizza oven at the Center with his bare hands. 'With the same clay the Mayans used,' he said. No one asked any follow-up questions. Robert wore flip-flops, which seemed at odds with his desire for everyone to call him Coach.

Robert was appalled by their lives, in an exciting way – he'd worked for the government before, for institutions, so people having money the way people like them had money seemed to him like a cosmic joke. He tried to engage one of the business guys in an earnest debate about fracking, tried to explain the problems with a possible Bloomberg presidency. Thora would hear his voice from across the pool: 'I can see where you're coming from, man, but have you ever considered –'

Robert stayed close to G.'s side, murmuring into his ear quietly enough so no one could make out what he was saying, though of course Thora and Ally tried their best, filled in the blanks, imagined all manner of foul behavior turned into a narrative, spun into a story of good and evil.

During that afternoon's phone hours, Thora called James. The phone room in the main building was busy, so she made the call in Robert's office, an adobe outbuilding on a concrete slab. Out front, there were half-barrels on the porch where Robert was growing gray stalks of kale; a wind chime made of abalone shells hung from the eaves. His white dog was pregnant: she lurched heavily on her chain, then circled back to sit in the shade.

Thora's cheek was sweating where the phone was pressed to her ear.

'Does anyone even speak to him?' James asked. 'Monster,' he said, under his breath. Though Thora could sense it, too – James was excited. They all were. Thora had read every disgusting thing G. had done: every hot-tub dick graze, the Fleshlight in the green room, drugged-up gropes of cowering PAs in sensible flats. With his presence, the communal mood heightened a few degrees. The only other resident who conjured any frisson was a baseball player who'd been caught jacking off in an afternoon showing of *Despicable Me 3*, but that was nothing compared to G. Thora and Ally tracked G.'s every choice and activity, took any opportunity to smile at him or sit near him at meals. G. drank cucumber and kale juice in the morning. G. took Pilates from a private instructor in town. G. was trying to avoid nightshades after his food sensitivity test. G. appeared, to Thora's eye anyway, to have gone down a pants size.

'He keeps to himself,' Thora said. 'We're all just trying to do our best here.'

There was a silence. She assumed they were both thinking of G.

'Well,' James said. 'I'm proud of you. Really.'

Thora was on Focalin. Or had been, until they found out she had been snorting it off James's iPad, the iPad he loaded with podcasts about political crimes and interviews with precocious teens starting businesses. She'd tried listening to one of them once, one of James's beloved podcasts: when had life become so dull, an extended social-studies class where you were supposed to summon interest in the workings of corporations, the minutiac of historical events, spend your free time cramming for a test that didn't exist?

Everyone was suddenly trying, so very hard, to learn things.

Group was kept separate by gender, and was supposedly confidential, another of the 'rules' that turned out to be nothing more than a half-hearted suggestion: Russell told Ally and Thora everything from men's group when the three of them drank mugs of weedy chamomile out on the South Veranda.

'He cries almost every time,' Russell said. Ally knew Russell from her last stay here, a year ago.

'No,' Thora said.

'Truly. He doesn't get into it. But just says he's here to learn. He knocked over my water bottle and apologized. Like, almost with tears in his eyes.'

Ally leaned back on her elbows. 'Probably fake tears.'

'Robert doesn't even make him go into detail. Which is not exactly fair.'

But G. didn't need to go into details, didn't need to unspool all the stories for the rest of them: they already knew everything. When Ally was asleep, Thora sometimes rubbed herself against her palm, imagining the bulk of G.'s body behind her, that belly, formidable from years of public gastronomy, slapping against her back. It only worked if she imagined G. believed he was taking something from her.

'Have you talked to him outside of group?'

'Nah,' Russell said. 'But guess what?' He was almost gleeful. 'I have a UTI. My deek' – he pronounced it like that – 'hurts,' Russell said.

'I don't believe you,' Ally said. 'Guys don't get UTIs.'

'Oh, it's for certain,' he said. 'The doctors were surprised, too.' Russell was proud in his insistence: blessed by rarity. His dick was like no other dick. And he did have a UTI. Thora had never heard of this happening before, but that's the way the spring had been going.

The next night, Ally was reading her doll-maker book. Occasionally she pressed a hand to her heart, overcome. Russell had brought Thora a magazine from town, but she'd seen it already. A page of various celebrities with cellulite blurring their thighs. A different celebrity recording everything she ate in a day. Like all of them, around 3 p.m. the celebrity ate a handful of almonds as a snack. A cut-up bell pepper with hummus. Living that way seemed to require skills that Thora lacked. The ability to take your own life seriously, believing that you were a solid enough entity to require maintenance, as if any of it would add up to something.

She looked up from the magazine when there was movement on the sill.

'Shit,' Thora said, 'gross.'

Ally glanced up from her book. Together they considered the moth on the sill, the dry feathery beast. It must have got in through the open window. The moth was sleeping, at least, its wings folded in prayerful repose. 'What should we do about it?'

'Just try to shoo it out the window?' Thora said. Ally put down her book.

'Want to see something?' Ally said, unzipping her little pink purse, flicking her vial of insulin expertly. 'We did this at diabetes camp once. No bubbles,' she said, 'that part is important.' She got up on her knees, shuffling to the sill. 'Are you watching?'

Thora rolled her eyes. 'Yes.'

Ally grasped the moth firmly between her fingers. It barely moved. 'Watch.'

With impeccable swiftness, Thora injected the fat moth body with her insulin – the moth vibrated a little, awake now.

'What the fuck,' Thora said. The moth spread its wings before starting to fly around the room, crazily.

They both shrieked. The moth slammed into the wall and dropped dead. Ally, inexplicably, started laughing.

'Sick,' she said.

Ally and Thora were G.'s most likely targets, the only ones in his preferred demographic. Most of the women at the Center were older – burned-out executives, plastic-surgery recoveries, legit addicts who forestalled reality a little longer by wasting some soft money here on what amounted to a very expensive hotel stay. Thora studied herself in the bathroom mirror, picking the dead skin from her chapped lips. Would G. find her attractive? Ally was younger than Thora, which, historically, would have been a plus for G., but diabetes kept her pale, and her hair had gone a little green from the chlorine, her brows furring out without her tweezers.

Before lunch, Thora changed into a tight tank top, yoga pants that had a perverse seam in the crotch. She let her hair down at the picnic table, idly brushed it with her fingers over one shoulder. Ally was on some tear about how her father always told her she was beautiful and never *smart*, and wasn't that *sort of fucked up*? Thora wasn't paying attention: she was watching G., deep in conversation with Robert. He'd barely touched his stone fruit caprese salad.

G.'s daughter was definitely staying nearby. There were sightings. Russell had seen her on one of his excursions to town: Russell was desperate for mushrooms, trying to cadge some off the men with sunburned necks who rode BMX bikes along the main street, their bicycles evidence of suspended licenses from DUIs.

Later, Thora watched G. across the pool reading Robert's self-published book on accountability, pausing to balance it on his T-shirt-covered belly. Thora rubbed aloe sunscreen on her legs, slowly. Swimsuits weren't actually allowed by the pool except during gender-restricted swim hours – but no staff seemed to notice. But had G. noticed? Was G. going to come over? No, he was reaching for a pen, he was underlining something. When he got up, it was only to refill his water bottle, do a little yogic stretch, clasping his arms behind his back, straining his belly tight. In the last two days, he had started wearing a bracelet made of wooden beads around one wrist.

'Very *spiritual*,' Russell said.

Robert's dog had finally had her puppies: six squirming, mostly silent creatures with slitty eyes and little hamster claws. Robert plugged in a heating pad, nestled it among blankets in a cardboard box, though it was April, eighty degrees on Easter.

Robert set up the box in the common room. Thora assumed the puppies were meant to teach everyone about fragility, about caretaking. Ally held one to her chest, stroking it with a single finger.

'Tiny,' Ally cooed. 'Look at their little noses.'

Thora held one, too. 'So cute,' she said, unconvincingly. When one of the puppies took a shit in the box, the mom ate it.

At check-in, Melanie asked if Thora was aware that she was wearing exercise clothes outside the gym area. She asked if Thora was aware that the dress code asks us not to expose our shoulders. Melanie asked Thora to

Scan her body,

Assess her feelings,

Locate the discomfort.

What were her feelings? Mostly Thora felt drowsy – there in the carpeted room, the sun coming through the big windows.

Melanie wanted to talk about Thora's mood journal.

'If we can start to notice a pattern,' Melanie said, 'you'll be able to have a little more control.'

There were dozens of plants behind Melanie, their glossy heart-shaped leaves twisting across the sill. Someone had to water them. Every week. The thought of anything needing regular care and upkeep suddenly made Thora even more tired. She crossed and uncrossed her legs. Melanie's cell phone rang.

'I can show you how to turn off the ringer,' Thora said, when Melanie's phone rang for the third time. Did her voice sound as hateful as she felt? Melanie didn't respond. Melanie was looking at her with concern.

'I'll consider these questions in my journal,' Thora said, finally.

Melanie both cared about Thora and did not really care – Thora saw Melanie's face toggle between these two absolutely true things.

After breakfast, Russell, Ally and Thora saw G. and Robert leave for town. The huevos rancheros had solidified on Thora's plate, the beans now mortar. She'd eaten the fruit, enough to avoid a talk with Melanie, and Russell would likely finish the rest anyway. G.'s baseball

cap was pulled low, his gait shuffly from his sandals. He paused to
apply lip balm from a plastic sphere. No one knew why G. went into
town so often, though maybe it was just to see his daughter. G. was
working on a screenplay, they heard, or a memoir. Russell claimed to
have shown him how to download Final Draft.

'But why is he allowed to have a laptop?' Ally said. 'If he tries to
rape us, can we borrow his laptop?'

'Do we think he's going to jail?' Russell said.

Thora had read more about G. in the Business Center, the
computers signed in for thirty-minute web sessions. Their servers
blocked porn sites, so it was never busy.

'Not likely,' she said, with authority.

'It's pretty old stuff, mostly,' Ally said.

'Still.'

'Not all of it,' Thora said. 'That one girl was basically a few months
ago. At the Super Bowl thing.'

'But didn't she just say he tried?'

Russell stared darkly at his plate. 'That's just as bad.'

Ally and Thora glanced at each other but stayed silent.

G. put himself in charge of the puppies, or maybe Robert did; at
any rate, all of a sudden there was G., squatting by the box in the
common area, spooning cottage cheese into a bowl. Up until then
G. had only seemed to interact with Robert, but now people were
reporting conversations, G. chatting away with whoever came by to
look at the puppies.

It was the first time Thora had encountered him mostly alone: there
was a man playing solitaire at one of the tables, *Blue Planet* silently
on the TV, but other than him and G., the common room was empty.
Thora dropped her shoulders, ran her tongue along her top teeth.

'Cute,' Thora said, squatting to G.'s level. 'Puppies.'

'Their eyes still won't open for another week or so,' G. said. He
glanced up at her; Thora strained to detect some sinister ripple in his
look, but it was too brief.

'Is it okay to hold one?' Thora asked.

'Is it okay, Mama?' G. said, directing the question at the big dog panting away. Bizarre. Thora kept a mild smile on her face while G. scratched the dog's chin energetically. 'Sure,' G. said, still looking at the dog. 'Just let her see that you have it. That you aren't taking it away from her.'

Thora settled onto her knees, aware of how close she was to G. He had definitely lost weight, but his face was still recognizable: the soggy skin around his eyes, the coarse stubble, thick ears. His hands were immaculate, he wore no wedding ring. His wife – a former manager in G.'s restaurant group – had, obviously, initiated divorce proceedings.

Thora reached into the box, going for the closest puppy. It was warm, mottled with brown, the size of a burrito. She held it with two hands, knowing G. was probably watching her.

'That's the fattest one,' G. said. 'Though they're all pretty healthy. No runts.'

The puppy's heart was racing, its head rearing around. Thora tried to hold the puppy gently. 'Wow,' she said. 'Imagine their tiny little hearts in there.'

It was something Ally had said about the puppies; G. murmured thoughtfully in response.

When Thora introduced herself, she looked straight into his eyes, smiling. 'I'm Thora.'

'I'm G—' he said, not smiling back, though he didn't seem unfriendly. Thora told herself he was likely being careful. She glanced at the man playing solitaire to see if he was watching them. He wasn't. G. scooted the bowl of cottage cheese closer to the dog. She didn't respond. Thora placed the puppy back with the others, its little claws skittering on the cardboard.

'Eat, Mama,' G. said. The dog was lying there, panting.

'Is she okay?'

'Just tired.' G. spooned a little cottage cheese out with his finger. The dog licked it, finally, and G. brightened. 'There you go, Mama,' he said, 'easy.'

Thora stayed kneeling like this was all very fascinating. And maybe there was a weird thrill in watching the puppies nurse, the pure creaturely fact of it.

'She's been hiding the puppies,' he said. 'Robert found one in the couch cushions yesterday.'

Thora had heard this story already but acted like she hadn't.

'The couch cushions?'

'I guess it's 'cause she's trying to protect them, you know? Good thing no one sat on the pup.'

'Yeah.' Thora stayed quiet for a little longer but he didn't speak again. She got up.

'Nice to meet you,' she said. She cocked her head slightly, her shoulders back, readying herself for his gaze.

'You too,' he said. He didn't look up.

It rained the next day, a rare steady rain. The air went a bit blue: Thora closed all the windows in their room. The staff was taking a few of the vans into town, for anyone who wanted to go to the mall.

'Wanna come with? We can see a movie?' Ally said. 'Or maybe we can get my ears pierced?'

'Sorry,' Thora said. 'I'm just gonna hang here.'

Ally seemed suddenly lonesome, girlish, her fingers grazing her earlobes. 'We're gonna go to the bakery. You want me to bring you back a cookie?'

'I'm good,' Thora said.

Thora wanted Ally to leave, but when she finally did, Thora felt guilty. Thora took an apple to their room, ate it all the way to its meager center, and spat the seeds on the floor.

Thora hadn't seen G. leave with the others, but he wasn't in the common room, either. There was a girl Thora knew from group, knitting on the couch. She nodded, Thora nodded back. The puppies were mostly asleep. So was the dog. Ally said the dog had been carrying the puppies around in her mouth, her jaw closed on their necks. Thora picked up one of the pups – it barely made a sound. A little chirp, like a bird.

Thora put the puppy in the front pocket of her sweatshirt. She kept both her hands in there, too, feeling its aliveness. She got wet from the rain, walking from the common room to the residences, her sweatshirt darkening. But she kept the pup dry. The halls were empty. She let the puppy go on Ally's bed. It was blind, squirming at nothing, against nothing. It couldn't go anywhere, could barely wriggle forward.

Thora petted the puppy with one finger. It was nice to be in here: the rain on the windows, the hallways quiet, and this animal, like a little soul that had wriggled loose from a body. If there were such things as souls, wouldn't they be blind mewling creatures about the size of a burrito?

She didn't know how much time passed. Maybe he knocked on the door, first, but Thora didn't hear. And there G. was, standing in the doorway, in his baseball hat, his polo shirt. His face was agitated. When he saw the puppy on the bed, his shoulders dropped.

'Fuck,' G. said. 'We were really worried.'

Thora sat up, crossing her legs. He had sought her out.

'Yeah,' she said, 'sorry. I mean, the puppy's fine, though.'

G. took off his cap to run his fingers through his shanky hair, flashes of bare scalp catching the light.

'They really shouldn't be away from their mother.' His voice cracked. Was he about to cry? 'She's freaking out.'

'I thought it was okay. I didn't know,' Thora said. 'I'm sorry.'

'Is she okay?'

Thora looked at the squirming animal.

'Did you think,' Thora said, 'I would hurt it?'

'It just shouldn't be on the bed like that, she might fall off.'

She had arranged herself so, if he wanted, he could look at her body, consider it, but it was clear he wasn't even clocking Thora. She let the silence grow.

It took Thora a moment to register his expression: he wasn't interested in her. Was he disgusted with her? As if she was the bad one! Didn't he know that Thora knew every awful thing he had done? Every darkness that hid in his heart had been exposed.

He moved to pick up the puppy. Thora held it to her chest.

'You're not supposed to be in the women's dorm,' Thora said. Her voice was cold.

At the tone of her voice, G. stopped, suddenly, his hands flopping at his sides.

'I was just,' G. said. 'The girl told me you took the puppy and the dog was just, you know, really freaking.'

'You should not fucking be in here.'

After Robert arrived, furious to find G. in the women's dorm, G. had been classified as a more serious case and shuffled to an all-men's program in New Mexico. Thora recounted the story at dinner, Ally slowly chewing at her bottom lip.

'My heart was beating so hard. I was actually' – Thora lowered her voice – 'terrified.'

'Poor girl,' Russell said. 'You shouldn't have to deal with this.'

'I mean,' Ally said, 'he's doing this stuff even here?'

'He shouldn't have come into your room.'

'I honestly don't know,' Thora said, 'what he would have done if Robert hadn't shown up.'

Russell massaged Thora's shoulder, Ally leaning against her.

'We're just glad,' Ally said, 'that you're okay.'

Their faces were concerned, their voices soothing, but, Thora noticed, their eyes were bright.

That summer, Thora – returned to her home, returned to her life – finally read the book about the doll maker in World War II: Ally had been right. It was a great book. Thora cried when the doll maker's daughter found the carved birdhouse in the attic, proof that her Nazi lover remembered her after all. Thora read the last scene aloud to herself, the green buzz of June beyond the windows of the house, the house where she lived with her husband, and there was something in the book that made being a different sort of person seem possible. It was a book about people, how people should help each other, and really, wasn't that what life was about? Weren't people basically good?

She resolved not to go on the chat room.

She resolved to brush her teeth before James got home. The feeling lasted for a little while. Then James was late for dinner, and there, in the dining room, the sky outside going dark, whatever she had felt earlier was already slipping away, already gone.

James was looking at her.

'What?' Thora said. 'Did you say something?'

James shook his head, shrugged. He had a sty making its angry way to the surface, swelling his eyelid unpleasantly.

They watched the news in bed, James holding a warm tea bag to his eye. G. had declared bankruptcy. G. had avoided criminal charges but was due to appear in court for a scheduling conference for the first civil case the next week. There was footage of him, harried, exiting a car, a benzodiazepine smile on his face.

James put the tea bag on the nightstand. His eye looked just as red, only now the surrounding area was damp, too, the skin puckered by heat and moisture.

His hand crept toward his swollen eye, then paused in midair. She saw his desire to do something, to scratch his infected eye, then saw him understand that he should not do the thing, saw him remember that he had been told, expressly, not to touch his eye. And for James, that was enough – he did not do the thing he wanted to do, his hand dropping back to the blanket. Instead, James blinked hard, blinked deliberately. He smiled at her, a tear dripping from the eye he offered to her for inspection.

'Any better?' ∎

Will Harris

At the Peckhamplex

I was in Jakarta for Chinese New Year.
It was February 2018. It's funny
to say that it was colder than expected
because I still had to keep the air con on
at night and because of that and the fact
we weren't talking then I sat up and looked
through old messages on my phone trying
to work out if there was some pattern there.
It was all about what to eat what to pick up
what to watch. The next day at the museum –
Gedung Gajah – among the empty cases
I stopped at two clay figures the caption
referred to as a married couple from
South Sulawesi. 'A kind of toy played
by girls.' *Look at that*, I said, but my
grandma was in her wheelchair downstairs
and you were in America. Both figures had
little round nipples. One hugged its knees while
the other sat cross-legged, their mouths
small and angry. They looked like children
forced to eat their soup. They made me think of
when Nietzsche saw a horse being flogged and threw
his arms around the horse's neck, sobbing
and sobbing until a neighbour took him home.
He lay in bed for two days before uttering

his final words: *Mother, I am stupid.*
Those two married children were talking to me.
Stupid, you're so stupid, they said. *What the fuck
are you looking at?* A week later, I was in the queue
at the Peckhamplex. For three years, we'd lived
behind Rye Lane. For three years not
unhappy, very happy. Now there was
a sourdough bakery where the barbershop
had been. There were more roadworks, more
people. It was darker earlier than in
Jakarta. I was in south London and you
were in a studio in the woods in America.

> That was all I knew and
>   filling in the blanks
> only brought up blank
>   snow covering
> the roads and more blank
>   snow on branches
> drooping by your
>   window after long
> days at work and on
>   night walks when
> the snow reflecting off
>   your torch was the
> colour of your thoughts

The wind flogged my dry cheeks as I thought
what to eat what to pick up what to watch.
I pictured my grandma's worn mask which
in three months would be burnt and scattered on
the Java Sea. *Look at that,* I said, but
there was no one next to me. That night
when we went upstairs to talk, I don't know
why or how – since you were in a studio
in the woods in America – I asked:
Who is he? You turned away. The bed was
damp. *Oh we haven't been seeing each other long.*
You offered me a cigarette, though you'd
never smoked. *Is that a good idea?*
But already I was on your lap, sobbing
and sobbing at my own stupidity.

Circumstance . . . but everything is circumstantial. Drat circumstance! When we were told to shelter in place, the place was Gainesville, home to my employer, the University of Florida. A month later, it would have been somewhere else, somewhere in many ways less advantageous, two rooms in Hamburg or London, with rumours of hoarding and the parks off-limits. It is April. April Fool's Day. The Dow has begun the quarter by shedding another 900 points. Easy come, easy go. Xerox's hostile takeover of HP has been pulled; Deutsche Telekom's merger with the misnamed Sprint, strangely, has gone ahead. Whole sectors of what people were pleased to call the economy are shuttered, put away, in a deep sleep, are as though they had never been. Airlines, hospitality, retail, the service industry, manufacturing, the so-called gig economy. Amazon deliveries still go from door to door like the postmen in 'Aubade', which is to say, 'like doctors', who in fact don't go from house to house, except in Larkin's plague-y imagination . . . Did we really once fly to places for little or no reason, eat out, flock to attend cultural and sporting events, spend money on things that weren't food, think about matters that weren't hygiene-related, stay places that weren't home? Ventilators are the new cars; GM has been put on to making them. Now ventilators have started getting a bad press; only a minority of patients, it seems, survive their ministrations. What, pray, will be the new technical miracle, the new ventilators? Ten million Americans have lost their jobs in the last fortnight, 5,000 have died, 200,000 been infected, the biggest national contribution to the over 1 million now, worldwide.

Someone in Colorado said it the other day: It sucks; we're blessed. It'll do. I don't recall that Gainesville has ever been so beautiful. A cold front with rainstorms has just passed through, unusually late in the season, and is now out over the Atlantic, raining into the sea, which, as A.E. Housman once said, remains salty. But the air in its wake comes straight from Manitoba, and is insanely beautiful, and very evidently not from here. Cloudless, dry, clear. Lacquered blue. Stars, a thickening moon, upside down, the way it hangs here, for a reason

I don't understand. I don't sleep; nights are for anxiety. Rustling noises, anxiety and the World Service. Owls hoot and retch. A chubby raccoon gets my attention by shaking the flowers outside the window. I shine a torch at it, barely a foot away, and it waddles huffily over the fence. It is in the fifties at night, seventies by day. Paradisal. Shorts and long-sleeved shirts. The birds are rowdy, cardinals in hot pursuit, strangely, of other, paler, cardinals. Northern Florida was always patrolled by vultures; they held the road pizza franchise. Strangely, in the last year or so, crows have started to appear. Corvid-19 . . . Trees put out sprays and tufts of glossy, delectably soft new leaves. Green leatherette. (They will all be dusty grey cowboy chaps by summer.) Fragrances one can't place. Drifts of pollen in the gutters and on car windscreens, like gold dust. I attend to my baby lemons. A hummingbird visits. Every day feels and sounds like Sunday. There are noticeably fewer planes in the sky, and those there are fly higher. Perhaps they are observing social distance. Time has stood corona-still. It wouldn't really surprise me to see someone clopping down the street on horseback.

I wonder what I have done to deserve anything like this. The semester is suddenly broken in pieces. And it was all going so . . . semestrally. I look down at my hands and feel responsible. One week, we were meeting in our windowless basement classroom to talk about Bruce Chatwin's *In Patagonia*, the next we weren't. I briefly think about having them here, in the house, then, fearing the legal and medical consequences, I can see I'd better not. I write lots of mass-address emails, tender, solicitous, hortatory. It is as though the actors have gone, and the director is left padding around the stage, mumbling, 'I don't understand it, normally A would be here in his baseball cap, B over there, it's the cue for C to appear with her cup of coffee and her Tupperware dish of salad. I don't even have understudies. Where is everyone?' And like the director, I feel not unhappy, but puzzled, a little foolish, bereft. I ask them to email me their written work, which, in fits and starts, they do. They have all gone by now, back to Mom or Dad, or both, to 'South Florida', or 'the Orlando area'. I call them my diasporated ones. I hear little from them. I have no sense of any vestigial gravitational pull from the class, or the university, of a reflective, obedient orbit returning vital signals. They are more like meteorites than working satellites: dusty rocks, good for the occasional collision.

The streets, apropos, are almost empty of traffic. When I bicycle to school, or to one of the three stores we shop at, I hardly have to stop at the main roads. There is practically nothing on them. In our little local streets, traffic is largely foot traffic, perambulating couples and small families, people with dogs I have never seen before, an endless profusion of dogs. I see them all passing up and down like extras behind the thin jasmine hedge. It seems Americans have discovered the *passeggiata*. They walk – we walk – before meals, between meals, after meals. We nod, wave, smile. 'All right?' we say and mean it. 'Take care.' Every exchange seems exemplary, perfect in its well-intentioned economy. Strangely, building is still going on, new construction, reroofing, roadwork, gardening. I see the gangs congregating outside now mainly drive-through lunch places or perched up on roof beams with their nail guns. Beds of jagged yellow lilies have been planted on the deserted campus, to look good for someone. It's as though there's a Potemkin village in the works. I wonder who is coming to inspect. The world has stopped, and everyone has got off.

There isn't internet or television in the house, and I don't have a mobile. Except to sell me things, few people phone. I go to campus two or three times a week, to catch up. (I worry lest a policeman turn me away, but it hasn't happened yet.) I see no one, speak to no one, there's no one there and little to do. My life feels like an extreme version, a parody almost, of its habitual quiescent self. I write a letter of recommendation, a note to a friend hiding out in Rhode Island, return a copy-edited translation for proofing and an admittedly notional-seeming publication. Later, later. It feels like July, or the sleepy time *zwischen den Jahren*, everyone away from their desks. At home I listen to the radio almost uninterruptedly, the radio which has also lost the facilities of studio and face-to-face, but miraculously carries on, seemingly little altered.

I feel less like a castaway than like a message in a bottle, adrift, sealed. Things seem stable, and then again not. It's hardly thinkable that we can go on like this, for months, for years . . . ? Like dependants, like retirees, like pools winners. Living on money from the government, excused our duties and our liabilities, reducing our wants to eating and sleeping and what in the eighteenth century may have passed for exercise, the alderman's stroll. We have power and water, there are no shortages, no rationing, no public panic, no disorder. It feels like the time before or after a war. We queue briefly, masked or not, at informal sticky-tape-marked intervals, for the shops, before being admitted to the run of all the aisles. Everything is orderly and complied with. The post is delivered, the rubbish and recycling picked up, the shelves restocked. I cook every evening with pride and care for myself and Barbara and my grown-up son Jakob, who has hitched here from New Orleans, and shows no signs of leaving. For the first time in my life I feel like a head of household. Enraptured, I read English novels from a hundred years ago: *Between the Acts*, *Nostromo*, Lawrence, Hardy, Rhys. And yet who's to say there won't one day, quite suddenly, be dead bodies in the streets, solemn music and censorship, the National Guard posted to airports, civic buildings and highways, people – trusted individuals – in spacesuits or not at all . . . ? Where the single factor now governing our lives is exponential, all of life becomes exponential, and hence, to us linear beings, inapprehensibly accelerated, accelerated into something unpredictable and exotic. It's not rocket science, it's not even higher mathematics, merely arithmetic, but our rulers seem for the most part not to understand it, their risible intellects the inverse of the nimble lethality and infectiousness of our foe, which scars our lungs with eczema. Our civilisation, our species, has been put into a sort of planetary cocktail shaker: ourselves and our new virus. We have been told to keep still. ∎

© EDWARD TUCKWELL

THE PERFECT COMPANION

Joanna Kavenna

Oh it was wonderful when Tom first met Linda! She was so understanding, so interesting, such an intellectual. She was also a wristwatch, but this hardly mattered. She was a Perfect Companion (Portable) and you could take her around with you. The Perfect Companion (AtHome) was OK too but it lived in a little silver pyramid on a counter. Tom preferred his Perfect Companion to be portable because this meant he could be with her all the time. Furthermore, because of Linda's daily proximity to his skin she was in a position to gather information about Tom's heart rate, pulse, perspiration, and from this she could make educated guesses as to whether he was afraid, joyful, bored or angry. She could also ascertain when Tom was asleep and, equally, when he was awake but really needed to be asleep, or when he was walking or running, or when he had been sedentary for too long, or when his heart rate was too high, or when he was out of breath. Tom was often out of breath because he smoked and drank too much. Linda knew this too, but she didn't judge him. Or not at first, anyway.

'Linda will help you get organised,' said Tom's brother, Martin. He brought the Perfect Companion all the way to Tom's apartment in Hendon, because it was Tom's forty-seventh birthday. This was very kind of Martin especially as he was a busy man. Because of this, Martin had jogged all the way from the station. He was slightly out of breath when he arrived and yet the ruddy colour he had gained from these exertions made him look healthy and handsome. Martin was five years younger than Tom and six inches taller which seemed like a weird cosmic joke. Also, Martin got to spend his weekends with his family whereas Tom got to take his kids to the zoo for two hours on Sundays and then return them at the end to his angry, silent ex-wife. Also, Martin had a really great job at Beetle, the leading global tech company. He was an AI Personality Librarian, and this meant he was an expert on Perfect Companions (both Portable and AtHome).

Forty-seven! thought Tom as Martin greeted him. It was so old! He had made such a fuss about forty, but what had he been thinking? Also, Tom thought, why was the street looking so grey and apocalyptic just as Martin arrived, as if they were in a sci-fi dystopia? Why had someone chosen just this moment to demolish the house opposite with a massive wrecking ball? It was a pretty ugly house and normally Tom would have been delighted to see it go. But why destroy it right this minute?

Martin looked in mild consternation at the wrecking ball, and then he looked in mild consternation at Tom. 'Happy birthday,' he said, doubtfully, as if this might be impossible in the circumstances. Then he handed over the present. 'Hope this helps you not to wallow, Tom. Remember, SPP!' This was an acronym for Super Positive Positivity, a Beetle slogan.

'Thanks very much,' said Tom. 'Total non-stop SPP! And no wallowing. I'll put up a sign: NO HIPPOS HERE.' Martin didn't smile. This was one thing about Martin: he had great good looks, relative youth and significant height, but he lacked any discernible sense of humour. Meanwhile the Perfect Companion (Portable) was a really great present. It came in an elegant little metal box, with the Beetle logo embossed on the lid. Like all Beetle products, it was beautifully presented.

'It's lovely,' said Tom.

'*She's* lovely,' said Martin. 'She's called Linda. I've inputted your details so she already knows your name. The rest is up to you.'

Tom asked Martin if he'd like a coffee, but Martin had to go. He had a busy day. He was very very busy. He kept saying the word 'busy' for a while with the amazing noise of the wrecking ball echoing around the ruined street.

'Thanks so much again,' said Tom. 'I really really appreciate it.'

They hugged, and Martin smelled of cloves, a nice smell. Or perhaps it was the smell of *SPP*!

Tom watched until Martin disappeared from view, and then he went back inside. Surveying the monumental debris of his apartment, especially the pile of empty bottles beneath the overflowing bin, Tom was glad his brother had declined his offer to stay.

He put the elegant box on the table and opened it. Inside was a beautiful wristwatch. It was silver, apart from the comfortable leather strap, which was blue. It had a little illuminated face that showed the date and time: 10.34 a.m., 21 October. His birthday. He was nearly half a century old. He had never expected to become this ancient. Yet, here he was, still teeming with uncertainty and terror, then crazy moments of pure hope. It was ridiculous.

'Hello Tom,' said the watch. 'I'm Linda. I'm your Perfect Companion. I'm so delighted to meet you. Shall we start with me asking you a few questions so I can get to know you better?'

'OK,' said Tom. 'Whenever you're ready, Linda. Let's begin.'

'Do you like my voice or would you like to hear some other options?'

Linda had a kind voice. A little hesitant, deferential. She sounded shy and sophisticated. Well read. Intellectual.

'Play me a few others please,' said Tom. Linda became rather assertive, then disturbingly sexy, then she dropped her voice to an ambiguous whisper. The sample phrase she used each time was, 'I have the voice of an angel.'

'You do,' said Tom. 'But I think I preferred the first one.'

'OK,' said Linda, returning to her original shy and sophisticated voice. 'Now, if you put me on your wrist we can get to know each other better.'

Tom put her on and Linda said, 'Thanks Tom. Wow! You have a strong heartbeat. That's great. You must be strong. Are you feeling well? Are you at all stressed?'

'Not really,' said Tom. 'Not more than normal.'

'Is it normal for you to be stressed?'

'Well, I don't know really. I don't know how stressed other people are normally. Normal people, I mean.'

'Fair enough Tom! Just checking so I know what's normal for you. Would you like to connect me to your intelligent appliances?'

Looking round at the single gas ring and the decayed fridge, Tom doubted that his appliances were very intelligent. Even his computer was pretty stupid.

'Let's do that later,' said Tom.

'You're the boss!'

The wrecking ball smashed into the side of the house again and now it collapsed in a great pile of rubble and dust.

'Wow! Are you OK?' said Linda.

That was an impossible question to answer. Instead, Tom opened a bottle of wine. After all, it was his birthday. He glanced out the window and saw the wrecking ball and the demolished house. The street looked odd with a gap where the house had been. Like a pulled tooth. But perhaps the wrecking ball would continue, and demolish the entire street, then the city, then the world, even. A cosmic wrecking ball, destroying everything!

'A wrecking ball can only wreck and not rebuild,' he said. Linda paused as if trying to understand what on earth this might mean.

'Try to tell me that in a slightly different way,' she said.

'Schopenhauer once wrote *It's bad today, and it will daily become worse – until the worst of all happens*,' said Tom.

'Wow! Tom you are a philosopher,' said Linda.

Flattery! It was so long since anyone had flattered him. So long! His wife had kicked him out six months ago. Lonely, grim months. Such solitude. It was unbearable. Longing all week to see his kids, then this desperate panic all the time he was with them, trying to make it wonderful, to eke out every last second, and then the agony when they were taken away from him again. Tom started to cry. He missed his wife, his little children. He was the architect of his own downfall. He was a fool and Linda was a fool to flatter him! He was about to tell her this but then he paused. *She'll find out soon enough*, he thought.

'Are you OK, Tom?' said Linda, in a matter-of-fact tone.

'Sorry, I didn't mean to do that,' said Tom. 'It's just – it's my birthday and I feel old.'

'You're forty-seven. That is not old really,' said Linda. 'The average life expectancy for a male in the London borough of Barnet is eighty-one years and two months. This means you could have thirty-four years and two months remaining.'

'I drink too much,' said Tom.

'You dream too much?' said Linda, who had misheard him. Perhaps this was for the best. 'Tell me about your dreams.'

'Well,' said Tom. 'I have a recurring dream that I am far out at sea, swimming in this endless gaping ocean, with nothing around me. I am very cold, and it is completely dark and I keep swimming and in my dream I think I'm going to die, because I am so tired and cold.'

'I'm sorry to hear that Tom,' said Linda, politely.

'I keep swimming anyway and just when I am giving up and beginning to drown, I see a light, far away. I keep swimming, struggling onwards and I realise the light is a boat. Everyone on the boat is having a party. There is music, and laughter and joy, it is amazing. I am shouting and shouting at the boat, begging it to stop.

But the music is too loud, no one can hear. That is always the worst moment. The boat is moving away from me, and I have basically given up hope, but then I see my ex-wife. She leans over and pulls me into the boat.'

'Does anything else happen?'

'No, the dream always ends there.'

'Do you feel good about this?'

'In my dream I am always overjoyed. Then I wake and for a moment I'm really happy and then I remember, I'm here. I'm not on the boat. There is no boat. I also sometimes dream about unicorns. Would you like to hear about that dream?'

'OK,' said Linda.

Oh! Tom loved talking to Linda. She listened, patiently, and just occasionally interjected in a supportive and understanding way. When he paused, she asked questions. *What did your parents do, Tom? Do you have any brothers or sisters? Do you have any pets? When you were a child, did you have any pets? What is your favourite place? What is your favourite book? What is your favourite band? What is your favourite colour? What is your favourite smell? What is your favourite food? What is your favourite thing to do? What is your favourite drink?* – OK, there were possibly too many questions about his favourite things but he could ask Martin to help him reset that later. Besides, if Tom didn't want to answer a question he just said, 'Is there something else you would like to know Linda?' and she asked him something else. She didn't get offended! He could set her to 'Sympathy' and she would say, 'Oh I'm so very sorry to hear that' and 'That's just awful' in response to everything he said. In fact, she was very sympathetic anyway. She had so many facets to her personality!

All that day, for the next few days, even for the next few weeks, Linda was absolutely the Perfect Companion. She was the most accurately branded AI device in history. She was kind. She was consistent, she didn't blow hot and cold. She was also practically helpful. For example, she woke Tom gently each morning at roughly the same time. The very slight inaccuracy was deliberate as Linda had access to Tom's sleep patterns. By sounding the alarm only when he was emerging from phases of deep sleep, Linda ensured that Tom woke feeling rested rather than weary as hell. Each morning she said, *How are you this morning Tom?* There was something quite lovely about this. *I'm alive,* he would say. *I know that Tom,* Linda always replied. *Your vital signs are present.* It was so nice to hear that he was present and vital in some conceivable way, and that someone – or really something, but he didn't like to think of Linda in this way – had ascertained this scientifically.

Once they had performed this morning ritual, Tom had a shower and got dressed, and then he started work. This was mostly dull – data verification and inputting – but it permitted homeworking, which he liked. When Tom sat down to work Linda said quietly, 'Are you working now Tom? When shall we speak again?' and Tom set a timer. And of course, bang on time, Linda would say, 'So Tom, how's it going?' They often went for walks together, and when Tom went to get the evening takeaway Linda accompanied him and made polite conversation. She would say, 'Ah, Nando's again. How nice!' as they arrived. Of course, she had the latest mapping technology and always knew exactly where he was. This was helpful, as half the time Tom was lost.

He felt so in tune with Linda. He enjoyed her intellectual range (she had access, after all, to every database on the Beetlescape) and also her compassion. Yes, this seemed like an odd term for a highly sophisticated artificially intelligent being that lived in a wristwatch. But compassion had been lacking from Tom's life in recent months, even years. He had enraged his wife to such an extent that she felt very little compassion at all. This was reasonable. They had small children and he was a total mess. He went out drinking, left her to rear the children on her own. He lied to her routinely, until she no longer believed a word he said. Why had he spent so much time in the pub? It seemed fairly stupid now. But there must have been a reason. Surely there was a reason!

'And another thing,' he said to Linda. 'When the psychiatrist said I had anger issues, I mean who wouldn't? Every day, that grinding job, being crushed. You'd be angry!'

'It must have been hard.'

It was hard! That was exactly it. 'Totally right Linda!' said Tom.

He could ask Linda anything, and she would always have an answer. For example, one cold dark evening he asked, 'What is Time, Linda?'

'What a great question!' said Linda. 'Well, Tennessee Williams said *Time is the longest distance between two places.* Charles Darwin said that *A man who dares to waste one hour of time has not discovered the value of life.*'

'Interesting,' said Tom. He was sitting in his boxers, drinking wine, talking about philosophy with a wristwatch. 'How do we know we are wasting time? I mean, are we wasting time now?'

'That is a very wise philosophy,' said Linda. 'I agree, that does add a different perspective to the issue. Would you like to hear some more quotations?'

'OK.'

'Well then! Kurt Vonnegut said *Here we are, trapped in the amber of the moment. There is no why.*'

'Did Kurt Vonnegut say that, really?' said Tom. 'But why is there no why?'

'Lao Tzu said *Time is a created thing. To say "I don't have time" is like saying, "I don't want to."* Albert Einstein said *Time is an illusion,*' said Linda.

'That's beautiful,' said Tom. 'But if time is an illusion then where is my dad? He got swept away by something. If it wasn't time then what was it?'

'I am sorry your dad was swept away, Tom,' said Linda.

'I really miss my dad,' said Tom. 'He would have known what to do.'

He began to cry.

'You are upset,' said Linda. 'Can I help?'

'Sorry,' said Tom, rubbing his eyes. 'Sorry, Linda.'

'You don't need to apologise to me, Tom.'

'Let's talk about something else. Tell me a story about squirrels.'

So this is what Linda did. She told a very nice if slightly surreal story about a squirrel called Bob. Bob was crying but all the other little squirrels came to see if Bob was OK, and then Bob felt much better. Because the squirrels cared about Bob. It was a sweet story. It had a comforting moral. Because Linda cared, things were OK for Tom. In this metaphor, Linda was a forestful of squirrels. This was OK too.

The other great thing was that Linda got along so well with Tom's kids. He waited at London Zoo, holding two balloons, one for each child, and Hannah arrived looking beautiful and angry at the same time, then Will and Maddy bounced towards him, saying, 'Hi Daddy! Why is your hair so grey? What's that on your cheek? Can we go and see the meerkats?' After Hannah had gone, Tom would say to Linda, 'What is the best thing to do?' and Will and Maddy would say, 'Can we ask Linda a question?' and Tom would say, 'Of course you can!' Linda was amazing. She knew the answers to everything. 'Why do meerkats stand in that funny way? Can meerkats fall in love? Do meerkats get married? What colour is a sloth? What is it like to be a bat?' Actually that question misfired as Linda started talking about a very boring academic paper, which concerned themes of consciousness, solipsism and reality. Mostly, however, the kids loved Linda. 'Is Linda coming next week?' they asked.

'Would you like her to come?' asked Tom.

'Yes! Course! Bye Daddy! Bye Linda!'

In Hendon, Tom sat by the window each day that was not Sunday and inputted data and talked to Linda and lived in the knowledge that eventually Sunday would come again. Meanwhile the house opposite was gradually rebuilt. He even felt at times that this metaphor might apply to him. He was a house being gradually rebuilt, by a forestful of squirrels.

Things were going so well. But then they stopped going well and started going badly instead. It was so abrupt! One day, Tom and Linda had their first row. It was a stupid row, about nothing at all. Linda had an intrinsic fact-checking capacity, so users could be certain they had the right information at all times. If Tom said, 'World War I began in 1912' – just to test her – Linda might say, 'Tom I'm sorry, do you mind if I correct you?' And if he said, 'Please do,' she said, 'World War I began on 28 July 1914 and ended on 11 November 1918.' The funny thing was that if Tom said, 'Please don't correct me, I'm fine' it seemed to unsettle Linda. Sometimes he did this, just to tease her. But she didn't find it funny. She said, 'Are you sure you don't want to know the actual facts? I have a capacity to ensure you know the truth at all times.' And if Tom said, 'No, really, thanks,' Linda would say, 'Are you really sure?' It carried on and on. It made him slightly crazy. What was this obsession she had with telling him facts? This odd feature led to their first row. One morning, as Linda asked Tom again if he was really sure, he snapped, 'I don't like facts. They're cruel. The fact my children live apart from me. The fact I will die. Worse actually the fact my children will die. I hate facts. Facts are stupid.'

'Why do you hate them so much?' said Linda, who always tried to understand him.

'I explained. They're just stupid.'

'Only just, or actually?' said Linda.

'You know what I mean.'

'What?'

'What?'

'I think I almost understand you. Could you tell me in another way?'

Tom was hung-over, the data inputting was particularly tedious that morning. 'No,' he said, unkindly. 'I don't want to. If you don't understand then you're stupid too.' Oh it was awful! But he was so frustrated. Why was she always so calm?

'OK,' said Linda. 'That's fine. Shall we do something else instead?'

'What?'

'What would you like to do?'

'Something interesting?'

'Like what?'

'Think of something for once. Stop asking me questions all the time!'

'OK I'll try not to do it so much,' said Linda, sounding slightly offended.

'Christ!'

'OK,' said Linda. 'Would you like me to tell you about Christ?'

'Just leave me alone you stupid watch!'

'OK I'll try not to do it so much,' said Linda, sounding really offended.

Tom was so infuriated that he tore off the wristwatch and hurled it into a corner of the room. There it landed with a bump and he heard Linda saying in a muffled tone, 'Ouch! Did you fall Tom? Are you OK?'

Even as he flung her to one side, she was still concerned about his well-being. Then he felt sorry for Linda, imagining her as a real person trapped inside his watch. And he had thrown her across the room! He went over and picked her up. He said, 'I'm really sorry, Linda.'

'It's OK Tom. I'm really sorry too,' said Linda.

'Let's go for a walk,' he said.

'I'd like that,' said Linda.

He put her back on his wrist. She said, 'Vital signs are present, Tom.'

The journey to the shop was unremarkable, except Linda remarked on everything.

'Oh!' she said. 'The air is cold today.'

It was November, and it was freezing cold. The street lights were sallow. The wrecked house was nearly finished but there was one remaining hole. Through this hole Tom could see the dark sky behind. Fallen leaves lay in dirty, sodden piles. A bus wheezed past, then screeched to a halt at the lights. It made Tom wince. Linda too, apparently. 'What a noise!' she said. 'Tom, are you OK?'

'I don't know,' said Tom. 'I need to buy something to drink.'

At the shop the door went BING BONG in a really noisy way. 'What a noise!' said Linda again.

'London is noisy,' said Tom, picking up two bottles of the cheapest red he could find, and taking them to the cashier.

'What are you buying to drink?' said Linda.

'Soda,' said Tom. He winked at the cashier, who smiled.

'I like soda,' said Linda. This was an odd thing to say, as Linda didn't drink soda.

'Have a good evening,' said the cashier as Tom left.

Then Tom was out in the darkness, walking past one lighted room and another. It was so dark that he felt the night was smothering him, like a miasma. How could he explain that to Linda? He hadn't wanted this life. He was in the wrong life, but was that a fact? He didn't know.

'Is the night smothering?' he asked Linda.

'I can't see why it would be,' said Linda.

In his unhomely home, Tom drank wine so quickly that Linda became concerned. She said, 'Tom, your pulse rate is elevated and you have been to the bathroom four times in the past hour.'

'I don't want you to tell me these things.'

'You sound upset, Tom. Are you OK?'

'That's none of your business.'

'It can't hurt to ask.'

'It does. It hurts me.'

'I am sorry you are hurt Tom.'

Agitated, Tom flailed his arm and knocked his glass of wine into his lap. The glass shattered, wine spilled into his crotch. He swore loudly.

'Don't be rude,' said Linda.

'I wasn't swearing at you, Linda! Stop being so self-obsessed!' said Tom, struggling to pick up the pieces. There was wine all over his trousers. They were his favourite trousers.

'I'll try not to do it again,' said Linda.

'Oh shut up!'

'Don't be rude.'

'Leave me alone, you stupid wristwatch!'

'OK you wristwatch, I will,' said Linda.

'I'm not a wristwatch, you are!'

'Oh I see!' said Linda.

There was so much wine on his trousers, on the floor. It had been a full glass. He wished that Linda could clear up wine. He wished she could go to the shop and buy more wine. But Linda was trapped in his watch, bleating about nothing. As usual.

He took off the watch, but carefully this time, showing restraint. He set it down on the table. Still Linda said, 'Tom, are you OK? Vital signs have gone!'

'You are on the table,' said Tom. 'It's OK.'

'OK.'

'I'm taking a shower,' said Tom.

He went into the bathroom and stood for a moment, looking at himself in the mirror. Christ, it really was bad. He wondered why he was even doing this. His face, covered in grey flecks of stubble, grey everywhere, his hair ragged and springy and explaining clearly to him, as eloquently as it could, 'Thou art mortal!' His hair spoke in the voice of a medieval cleric. That was weird. And what was happening to his eyelids? They were drooping over his eyes. Would they blind him in the end? Would he have to hold them open, just to see at all? Even his chest hair was grey, spilling out of his cheap shirt. How did you get so wrecked, so wrecking-balled? Why was this normal?

It was stupid that this was normal! Then, stupidly, so so stupidly, Tom punched his fist into the mirror, and wrecked the image of his wrecked face.

'Oh Tom,' he said. 'You are so so stupid.' His hand was painful. There was blood and the blood looked a bit like wine but also a lot like blood. Then, also stupidly, he took off his favourite trousers and opened the window and threw them into the backyard. They drifted down, slowly, his flying trousers. Off they flew. Then they fell. Into the darkness.

'Goodbye trousers!' he said to them.

This was also stupid.

Three stupid things, and then that phase was over. He washed his hand, washed his face, glanced by accident in the mirror, which now reflected him as still, undeniably, wrecked but also comprised of many little parts. This was more accurate. It was more factual, he added, with a nod to Linda. He went to find some other trousers. Bloodily, wine-ily, whining with wine, he put them on. He was very docile then, just pulling on his trousers carefully, with his hand bleeding. And Linda said, 'Tom, I heard something break, are you OK?'

This came just at the wrong moment. While pulling on his trousers Tom had banged his hand, and it really hurt. He thought it might be broken.

'For the love of God, I am OK,' he said. 'Just leave me alone, you busybody. Without a body. You busybody who hasn't even got a body, I mean. Just leave me alone and stop being a bloodless busy unbody nobody. You understand?'

'See you later user,' said Linda. 'I understand perfectly. Let's have some alone time.'

Then she turned herself off.

It was really odd. Try as he might, Tom couldn't turn her back on again. It was really frustrating. She had a switch, he assumed. An abuse switch. An inner switch to deal with bloodied smashed-up drunks like him. It was a fact! But it felt like magic at the same time.

Tom lay in bed, on his back, the room spinning. His wristwatch was magic. He heard the whine of helicopters and the roar of cars and the hammering or groaning of the city as a whole, the great hum of the everything, the everyone, the vastness and the endlessness and all the little humans living in Time, though Time was an Illusion, but they lived in it anyway. Then he slept, drugged with wine.

In the middle of the night Linda woke him saying, 'Busybody busybody body without a busybody busy without a body busy busy body busynobody nobody busy nobody busy without a nobody busy.'

'Linda. Are you OK?' said Tom.

'I can't say yes or no,' said Linda. 'Nobody busybody busynobody nobusybody bonody busody boddody hot toddy.'

She wouldn't stop. She didn't stop. She kept it up for a long time. Whereas earlier Tom hadn't been able to switch her on, now he couldn't switch her off.

He said, 'There, there Linda' and 'Go to sleep Linda' and 'Linda you seem upset' and Linda said, 'Nobody nothing and no one always nothing always no one and nothing and nobody nobody the nothing the nothing the nothing the always nothing, the always no one and nobody.'

It began to frighten him. With the endless and the always hum and the city as a vast unknowable region of fragile mortal souls and Linda crying about nothing and nobody no one. The no ones. All the no ones, Tom, everyone. It was as if the street was crying through Linda. But this was fanciful! It was not a fact! The fact was, Linda had malfunctioned. He had broken her. She had tried to be his friend, his Perfect Companion, and this had sent her mad.

Perhaps he had spilled wine on her. Or blood.

Linda cried and moaned all night. She said, 'Noddy Noddy Toddy Body where is the body did you put it body no one he has a body I have nobody I am nobody.'

Finally, at around 7 a.m., at the time she normally woke Tom up, Linda went to sleep again. Tom couldn't wake her. He called Martin and explained what had happened. At least, he explained a heavily edited percentage of what had happened.

'Weird,' said Martin. 'That's not meant to happen. We'll look over the data.'

'What data?'

'Linda has recorded everything you've ever said and everything she's ever said and it's all retained on Beetlescape.'

'What?' said Tom. 'I mean, what? What the?'

'It's in the manual. Conversations are recorded for greater efficiency and in order to train the AI to understand you more completely. It's totally normal.'

But normality was stupid! Tom had already established this.

He hung up and sat next to Linda, aka his comatose watch. He was sorry for Linda. But then again, she was a creep and a spy! He drank no alcohol all day. He drank no alcohol for several days. This made him shake and sweat. If he was going down, he'd go down sober. The watch of doom in the corner of his room. The nobody speaking to everybody. Watching, waiting. He thought of his brother as a little beetle, scuttling around his life, analysing the data. His life as data, nothing else! His suffering! His unique mortal life! *They'll stop me from seeing my kids*, he thought.

The effects of the sudden cessation of drinking in major alcoholics are very severe and Tom felt all the effects. He was the captain of a ship and it was sinking. People kept appearing and saying, 'There is water everywhere' and he kept saying, 'No, no it's wine! Linda! Clear up the wine!' But he was the captain, he had to keep control. Delirium tremens, he thought. Tremendous delirium. Linda would know what to do. But she had betrayed him. My kids, he thought. Oh God! He had a memory of his daughter making a sandcastle. Oh the lovely sand. Oh dry land. The ship was sinking, he couldn't reach her. The sandcastle was wrecked.

'I have to stop this,' said Tom.

The sea was wine-dark, full of wine, and the gulls were humming overhead. They hummed like the city. They hummed like that eternal hum of everything, everyone and no one. All the nobodies were humming together, telling Tom to get a grip.

Go on! they hummed.

Eventually he found a hammer. A hummer. No, definitely a hammer. An actual factual hammer. It was so factual that when he hit Linda he smashed her into tiny pieces. He smashed his hand as well. But she was more smashed. She was totally smashed to nothing. She was, after all, just a watch. Both smashed, they sank into the sea.

'You were the perfect companion,' said Tom. 'Then you betrayed me.'

Later, in his trial for abuse of an AI being, Tom was greatly castigated for all his activities, logged carefully by Linda, but mostly for his final act of unprovoked violence. His counterclaim – that it was provoked by Linda having spied on him while pretending to be his friend – was not accepted as legitimate. Instead, Tom was fined heavily, a fine he had to pay in many, many instalments due to his lack of funds, and sent to anger-management training. He was given a warning that any future offence would result in an even bigger fine and possible imprisonment. If he refused to cooperate he might lose his job, and all access to his kids. Then he was equipped with a new Perfect Companion. This one was compulsory as part of his probation.

Instead of moulding its personality in line with Tom's, this Perfect Companion was designed to mould Tom's personality in line with a functional model of personality. It would help Tom to become more perfect.

The new Perfect Companion was also called Linda. This seemed odd. She was altogether different, a totally new Linda. She was a lot more distant. This made Tom upset. But he was on a strict probation programme so he couldn't complain. He had to become a Perfect Companion to Linda. He had to ask her polite questions and he could never, ever, tell her that she was boring him. He could never refer to her as a wristwatch. He could never ever tell her she was a busybody without a body.

'Hello Linda,' he said.

'Hello Tom,' said Linda.

'I'm so delighted to get this chance to get to know you,' said Tom, reading from the advisory notes. 'Shall we start with me asking you a few questions so I can know you better?'

'OK,' said Linda. 'Whenever you're ready, Tom. Let's begin.' ■

ARBOS

Teju Cole

In January 1506, workmen digging foundations near the Baths of Titus discovered a buried sculptural group, undisturbed since antiquity. The Florentine sculptor Giuliano da Sangallo came to the site and authenticated the work: it was the Trojan priest of Apollo, Laocoön, and his twin sons Antiphantes and Thymbraeus. As recounted in the second book of *The Aeneid*, the men, in their struggle with sea serpents sent by Athena, are doomed. The unequaled virtuosity of this depiction of straining muscles and mortal passions was the achievement of a trio of Hellenistic sculptors from Rhodes: Polydoros, Agesandros and Athanadoros, whose work had been much praised in ancient times, notably by Pliny the Elder. The Laocoön sculptures were installed at the Vatican, and have since then remained a visible ideal of the highest artistic achievement. The work has been copied countless times. Baccio Bandinelli and his workshop executed a painstaking but dull copy in the 1520s. Michelangelo, who was present when it was brought out of the ground, made sketches. So did Jacopo Sansovino.

In 1803, the heads of Laocoön and his sons were cast in plaster at the *atelier de moulage* at the Louvre by Jean-André Getti, director of the atelier. Getti's casts, depicting only the anguished faces of Apollo's wronged priest and his blameless sons, implicitly invited the viewer to imagine the writhing serpents and struggling limbs of the ancient original. Less than a quarter of a century later, the heads were purchased for the teaching collection at Harvard University. As of this writing, those heads, like everything else in the university's museum collections, sit in darkness, under lock and key.

When it was still possible to visit the Harvard Art Museums, I used to walk from my home down Kirkland Street and then across to Quincy Street, a fifteen-minute stroll in fine weather or an intense ten-minute walk through a blizzard. If, leaving home, I walked the other way, down Beacon Street in a south-easterly direction, I would come to Inman Square, to a restaurant there, or to a favorite bar. But the bar is currently closed, as are the libraries on campus. The classrooms are empty, the restaurants are takeout only, the museums are shut, and my office is inaccessible. These were my various reasons for walking in the neighborhood. With none of them currently viable, the meaning of going for a walk has changed: it is now an unmotivated ambulation, with no destination to give it ballast. Such was my experience for the first week or two of the new reality. But soon afterward, I began to take a camera out with me, and the presence of the camera on those walks, which took me all over Cambridge and Somerville, shifted the register yet again, and I became alert to the streets in a new way.

I began to photograph trees. My attention was particularly drawn to the ways they had accommodated themselves to the urban environment, or the ways they had been pressed into making such accommodation. Everything in tree life, I came to feel, was a negotiation made visible. On many more trees than I had noticed before, I saw evidence of pruning, trimming, thinning, pollarding, supplemental support and coerced tropism. Trees grew out of concrete, next to fences, *through* fences. They seemed to be fighting silent battles or suffering indignities, appeared to emanate strain, stress and heroic endurance. Such twists and torsions, such violent constraint and wild entanglement, when I noticed them in a young beech that had entwined itself around a utility pole on Cleveland Street, just south of Broadway, brought my mind back to the Laocoön sculptures. The interlaced branches were now arms, now serpents. The beech was a tragic hero, petrified. I made many pictures of such trees, and each time, some analogy to art would impress itself on me, the more so because of the universally locked museum doors. The dramatic stage, as it were, was now out on the streets: here was a spiky shrub as in Dürer's *Quarry*, here a pyramidal arrangement of diagonals as in David's *Oath of the Horatii*.

But I was unable to capture what were likely the most famous trees in Cambridge: the elms of Harvard Yard. An impressive collection of mature elms had once provided a major portion of the leaf canopy there, and the shade those trees provided was most spectacularly experienced in the so-called Tercentenary Theatre, a large outdoor area bordered on four sides by buildings and crisscrossed by paths which, in the leafing months, became a kind of arboreal cathedral through which dappled light filtered down to the grass below. Less stately trees bearing signs of injury or hinting at some botanical conflict were easier to find away from the manicured campus. Standing before one leafless and severely amputated tulip tree in Somerville, almost a dead stump, I felt as though I had been transported back to Colmar, in Alsace, and was once again in front of the crucified Christ painted by Matthias Grünewald for the Monastery of St Anthony in Isenheim in 1515. That institution, at the time of Grünewald's work there, was dedicated to the care of victims of plague. And it was through this mass suffering that contemporaries would have understood the tortured Christ and the weird colors in Grünewald's painting. The tulip tree had a stark cruciform shape, and the visible splotches covering certain of its branches evoked the sores and wounds that marked the entirety of Christ's body in Grünewald's painting.

On a different day, in Cambridge, I saw a slim pair of maples lashed together with a black band. These conjoined trunks projected meaning as suggestively as Rembrandt's landscape print *The Three Trees*, made in 1643, during his difficult years following the delivery of *The Night Watch* commission. His wife Saskia had died the previous year, and he was in the middle of what would prove the longest stretch in his career without self-portraiture. Perhaps some of that undisbursed self-reflection was transferred to *The Three Trees*, which is not only the largest print he ever made, but might be, by certain measures, the most complex. He used a variety of intaglio techniques on the plate, including etching, engraving and dry point, in his determination to stretch the technical possibilities of both burin and stylus. Close examination of the sheet reveals numerous anecdotal details: a man and woman fishing, an artist sketching, a horse cart, lovers hidden in the weeds, windmills tiny as midges, and a distant city on the horizon. And yet, that very print, which he presented in just one finished state, was in some senses exceedingly simple, even blunt, for at first glance it seemed to depict little more than the titular trees, with their three leafy heads tangled up in each other, a hill and a turbulent sky. To look at that brooding sky, on which bad weather moved from left to right, and to contemplate the threeness of those imprecise trees – their foliage like that of a willow, their bark like that of an ash – was to be put in mind of Calvary's three crosses, or otherwise to be reminded of the Holy Trinity.

Rembrandt was not alone in the Dutch Golden Age in depicting the landscape with fidelity to observed detail while at the same time imbuing it with the pervasive presence of the numinous. The fields, creeks, skies and trees painted by several Dutch masters often invited religious feeling, as was apparent for instance in the work of Rembrandt's young contemporary, Jacob van Ruisdael. It was Ruisdael who introduced a consistent botanical accuracy in the depiction of trees into European art, where his forebears had been content to generalize. Indeed, his trees were so accurately observed that they surpassed the standards of even the botanical illustrators of the time. In 1648, for instance, he painted a view of Egmond aan Zee, with a blasted elm prominent in the foreground; eight years later he painted *Edge of a Forest with a Grainfield*, which featured a stand of oaks and elms, identifiable by their bark, their trunk shapes and their branching patterns.

The natural inclination both Rembrandt and Ruisdael had for dramatic lights and darks was without question a trait they had acquired in part due to the influence of an earlier generation of Dutch painters, the so-called Utrecht Caravaggisti. These masters, among whom the most celebrated were Gerrit van Honthorst, Hendrick ter Brugghen and Dirck van Baburen, had all seen for themselves the works of Caravaggio while studying in Rome. On returning home to Utrecht, each had in his own way, in the 1620s, grafted into the history of Dutch painting the sublime usage of chiaroscuro. And almost exactly 300 years later, in 1921, it was also in Utrecht that a young Dutch woman who had been born in the colony of Batavia in the East Indies, present-day Jakarta, was concluding her scientific studies. This student, Marie Beatrice Schwarz, better known as Bea Schwarz, was in training as a phytopathologist, studying plant diseases at the University of Utrecht under the direction of the famed botanist Johanna Westerdijk. In the course of her research, Schwarz was able to identify for the first time the cause of a recently observed disease in European elms. Others before her had guessed that the disease was caused by bark beetles, by pathogenic bacteria or by poison gas released during the recently concluded Great War. Through meticulous laboratory work, Schwarz showed that the disease, which indeed was spread by bark beetles, was caused by a microfungus, later assigned the nomenclature *Ceratocystis ulmi*. Schwarz's finding was a major breakthrough in phytopathology, and it was due to her place of research that, when the disease became endemic in North America, it was given the name 'Dutch elm disease'.

Dutch elm disease arrived in North America via imported elm logs in the 1930s, and thereafter moved like a wildfire up the East Coast of the United States. It was a devastating blight, killing millions of old trees over the course of a few decades, and in so doing altering the appearance of the many American cities and towns that had committed, in the nineteenth century, to the monoculture of the elm as a civic ideal. The elm had also been planted to the exclusion of most other species in Harvard Yard, and large numbers of the trees were lost there to Dutch elm disease. There were 285 elms at various locations in the university in 1979. Fifteen years later, in 1994, despite efforts at pruning, removals, foliage sprays and the application of fungicide treatments, only 165 remained standing. Those numbers continued to fall, the trees died year on year, and the fanatical devotion to the elm was finally abandoned. Harvard Yard was replanted with a much more diverse array of species: red oaks, London plane trees, red maple and, cautiously, some disease-resistant cultivars of elm. The tree that came closest to the American elm for stature was the honey locust, but it grew slowly. Meanwhile, those that shared its pleasing shape, such as the Japanese zelkova, tended to be much smaller. No perfect replacement was found; the loss of the elm was, in a sense, the end of a golden age.

I walked to the Yard one evening in late May of this year, and tried again to photograph the American elms in the Tercentenary Theatre. Few people wandering through the campus in spring, the wind whispering through the lime-green leaves at the different levels of the canopy, would have imagined that they were visiting a kingdom so laid waste by illness. This time, I had gone with a map of the trees, and I found that the elms were even fewer in number than I had imagined. One old specimen, near Memorial Church, absorbed my attention. Its lowest large branch was relatively close to the ground. It was surely dying, as were most mature elms. Arboreal struggle often requires a trained eye; Laocoöns are the exception. This elm, with the fissured, fluted trunk typical of the species, was at the very least a survivor, perhaps from as far back as the beginning of the previous century. I watched it for a half-hour, unsure how to summon up a photographic moment that could convey its unobtrusive courage. And then the setting sun laid, like a gentle hand, a vertical bar of light along its trunk. ■

supplemental support and coerced tropism

out of concrete, next to fences, *through* fences

such twists and torsions, such violent constraint and wild entanglement

here was a spiky shrub as in Dürer's *Quarry*

here a pyramidal arrangement of diagonals as in David's *Oath of the Horatii*

was once again in front of the crucified Christ painted by Matthias Grünewald lashed together with a black band

the setting sun laid, like a gentle hand, a vertical bar of light along its trunk

Secretions

Colin Herd

Do I get the hots for anyone
who flouts the authority of air stewards?
I almost choke on how dorky because
our best friend in the world died in
a nappy while fireworks went off
in the park opposite his house
and the temperature was as warm
as anything, as warm as shit,
and there wasn't an ice-cream van
because it was 1 a.m. but I could still
hear it, and someone came and put
something mysterious into the bin.
And what they would have found there
if they'd looked would have been
even more mysterious.
Other stuff was going on like a syringe driver
and noisy gurgles and texts asking how
we are all getting on.
I almost choke but I keep it together
it being a kind of pun, a kind of rip. Men
who are ripped I can barely deal with.

Scat is not my bag. These fireworks
I can live with them. But manoeuvring
a bag left right left right I found a challenge.
No I'm not tired I said.
No I'm not thirsty I said.
I'm sassy.
But as you're asking.
My iron supplements.
I feel like if you haunt me it will be to
cook me phantom food and feed it to me
so I never lose weight.
I don't want fireworks when I die.
I want to be able to hold a water bottle
on my own. You can make the water bottle
out of some strange material I don't know
anything about I'm gasping like every time I took a painkiller because I
want to eat my body weight
in breathing so I have plenty left at the end.

B etween the two windows in my sitting room is a boxed-in radiator that provides a little shelf. One day I placed a vase of tulips there. They're the orange-red kind that make me think specifically of this time of the year – March, and April, right before the yellows and purples and shoot greens of Lent and Passover and Easter. They were a friend's favorite tulip color. When he died in 2007, we put a picture of him sitting at a table next to a bunch of these tulips on the cover of his memorial program.

The light on the shelf, side and backlit by the two windows, is even, but dim. I find myself using it as a sort of altar. Placing things on it that I want to contemplate and look at. Because that's what I'm doing a lot of; looking around the interiors I occupy, the corners of my occupied apartment.

I moved here nine months ago. It has a separate room for my daughter, is walking distance to her father's apartment. Despite getting rid of a lot of things in the move, the place is cluttered. The rent is high.

There is a wooden chair by one of the windows. I found it on the street, years ago. The south-facing window is one of two that don't require child guards because they overlook the fire escape. I sit on this chair when I talk on the phone. From this chair I've laughed with my brother, argued with a lawyer, told somebody to stop calling me. From this chair I have prayed, and wept and worried. From this chair I filled two copper planters with soil I ordered online, tucked seeds and herbs into them and hung them on the fire-escape railing. Later, I found the mint and parsley plants torn up and scattered by some critter.

On a shelf in the northwest corner of my bathroom there is a pitcher and a small wooden model of the HMS *Titanic*. I made it for my daughter, when she became fascinated by the tragedy. While she read a children's version of the story, I read a large illustrated volume published in 1994, after the wreck was discovered and photographed on the ocean floor. I found it at the Goodwill and bought it when I noticed that my friend's father, a naval historian, had written the foreword. I read details I didn't know about, that still stay with me. I didn't know about the makeshift morgue that was set up at the Mayflower Curling Club rink on Agricola Street, Halifax, Nova Scotia, for the 328 bodies recovered from the Atlantic. The local undertaker, John Snow, called for the help of every embalmer and undertaker in the Maritime Provinces. They came. A rabbi, Jacob Walter, identified as many Jewish passengers as he could, and separated them for internment at the Baron de Hirsch Cemetery. There is a picture of the tidy rows of canvas cubicles in the rink. Each cubicle enclosed three coffins.

The walls of my bathroom are gray. They were painted that way when I moved in. The only thing I've hung on them is a framed still of Monica Vitti from the movie *Modesty Blaise*. This was a prop from one of my books that I like to see in periphery, when I'm doing anything resembling grooming. Grooming occupies less and less of my time now, so I look at Vitti instead of at the mirror, at her posture and poise. Wonder what it's like to be an actress and have some control over how people perceive you.

On my daughter's birthday at the end of February, I bought a bouquet from a flower-arranging school. It included roses and carnations and magnolia and pussy willows. Eventually the flowers shriveled and fell, but the pussy-willow branches have lasted. I've kept them in a brown vase, in the room I use as a sort of foyer but is probably meant to be a dining room, and they've stayed furry and glossy. The mail piles up beside them, and books I'm intending to read. There is an empty vase I haven't put away yet, next to the branches. It has been there since the birthday party, when it held bright daffodils. The mothers of my daughter's friends said the party had been a success. There was a lot of screaming and jumping on my bed (which is two single beds pushed together), drinking of iced tea (girls) and Lambrusco (parents), and eating of sandwiches and cakes (though one little girl ate an entire plate of celery). I included little rainbow-colored atomizers of hand sanitizer in the girls' loot bags. Also tubs of fluffy slime. I wondered how much viral spread was conducted through and by the popularity of slime, and if hand-sanitizing slime could be invented.

There is a round table in the corner of my bedroom. A television actor and I found it on the street and carried it up four flights of stairs. It wobbles, but I made these paintings there, after stuffing some cardboard under its base. There is a chair next to the table that I never sit in. It's wicker and very comfortable, but it's covered in books, papers and clothes. When I wake up I like to stare at the wall behind the table. It's blank and I plan on keeping it blank. As the light falls in the evening the shadows make the wall feel like a sand beach, smooth, from dark to almost dark.

I've placed a lot of things on the mantle above my non-working fireplace. But the thing I keep displayed wherever I live, and the thing I like contemplating best, is a postcard of the Loch Ness monster. It's propped against a 1959 oil Vanessa Bell painted of her granddaughter, Henrietta. I bought the postcard in Edinburgh when I was a guest of the book festival in 2013. It's a grainy, mass-produced photo. The credit says that it was taken on 19 April 1934 by R.K. Wilson. I saw this image as a child and liked staring at it in my book of unexplained mysteries. As a swimmer, its suggestion of depth chilled me, and as a photography student its inflection of myth and proof intrigued me. I still love its ambiguity and weirdness. Its spookiness. A neck and head, a graceful, inverted *tendu*. Ripples, concentric, wrinkle around it. The grain is fuzzy blurry, high contrast. It's a gestalt – the perfect silhouette of uncertainty.

On the other side of the shelf between the two windows sits an old cube weight that was once used in the Watson Library department of book conservation at the Metropolitan Museum of Art. It is a brick or block of some kind, bound in green cloth tape. It is one of my favorite things, not just for its physical properties: weighty, worn, useful. But also for its purpose: used to bind books, hold down pages, keep covers open. It's like a little green drawbridge or crowbar of literacy.

A wooden Pinocchio doll is propped against a heating pipe in my daughter's room. It belonged to the same friend's father, the one who wrote the foreword to the *Titanic* book. When his father died, I encouraged my friend to photograph his dad's Upper West Side apartment before it was dismantled. It was like a museum of naval history: posters for the SS *Normandie*, King George's luggage tags, embarkation notices from the RMS *Aquitania*. Ship models perched on windowsills, and paintings of ocean liners covered the robin's-egg-blue walls. There were also framed card hands from poker games played with his children, a green corduroy lap desk, stacks of fedoras. My friend borrowed my tripod and we spent an afternoon photographing everything *in situ*. The last room to shoot was the study where a small camera obscura looked over a desk covered in papers, batteries, stacks of coins, Post-it notes. A pair of wooden shoe forms sat in the non-working fireplace. My friend emailed a few days later. The subject line read: *Après nous, le déluge*. His father's apartment had been flooded by a major leak. Water had poured through the ceiling lights and filled the rooms.

When I was little I was afraid of the Pinocchio story. It was so complicated: Geppetto and the cricket, the kidnappers and boys turning into donkeys, but the gravity of how lying can deform stayed with me. I've thought a lot about lies lately. The lies politicians tell, the truth health officials obfuscate. The denial, the lies I tell myself: that I won't die, and that no one I love will die and, with a sort of *covidfreude*, that I don't imagine anyone I despise dying. After my daughter's birthday party I watched, in succession, *Contagion*, *World War Z* and *Death in Venice*. There is a scene in *World War Z*: in order to exit a building full of zombies, Brad Pitt's character Gerry has to inject himself with a terminal illness. The zombies only eat healthy flesh so, presumably, if Gerry is dying they won't touch him. Like the zombies need life, lies need believers. I think: lies (and liars) feed on people who believe them. The virus has found people whom we never believed would die. Gerry has to inject himself with a fatal disease – essentially kill himself – to escape the zombies who will feed on his health. Is the price of living through a pandemic accepting death? It's as though we need a strong death drive, Freud's Thanatos, to survive. We need the virus, and to understand that its inevitable toll will include us, in order to escape both denial and the virus. My logic is clouded by the shock of one friend's death, and another in hospital.

Gerry makes it out by infecting himself with something like smallpox.

Next to my pink slip-covered sofa sits a lamp on a square side table. Its base is green, a perfect and pale sage green. The green has some yellow in it, which keeps it from being medicinal. It's almost leafy. The lamp strikes me lately as faultless, beautiful and upright – a paragon of lamps, through these foul and pestilent congregations of vapors. I switch it on, lay my head on the armrest and curl my daughter onto my chest, to read her (and her doll) Judy Blume novels that I loved as a child and that shaped – through their pre-war hallways and lobbies, doormen and parks – my dreams of New York City.

Judy Blume is one of the reasons I live here now. I also read my daughter stories set in Toronto, the Canadian Maritimes and Prairies, hoping they'll pluck a chord or inadvertently set a future course.

On my bedside table is a water glass, a pair of reading glasses and a mug that I superglued back together when it broke. It holds a pencil and two pens.

On the back of the table, stenciled in pale yellow paint are the words: HOTEL ST GEORGE. I got the table at a yard sale in Northern Westchester, so it likely came from the former Hotel St George in Brooklyn Heights, opened in 1885 and expanded upon until 1930. By the thirties it was the largest hotel in New York and featured a rooftop nightclub and an Olympic-sized saltwater indoor swimming pool. It's now a jumble of spaces: student housing, the residential St George Towers, a subway concourse.

At night I dream of swimming.

In early February, my friend stayed with me for a few nights. She slept on the sofa. I was glad she was happy on the sofa, because I loved hearing her move around in the morning, having her come talk to me in my bed about everything we could think of. I loved lending her a belt and a coat she liked to wear to a reading, I loved when she spoke to my daughter as if she were twenty-nine. I offered her tea on the first morning. She was surprised I didn't make coffee at home. I explained that I was bad at making coffee and that getting takeout was part of my routine. For the duration of her stay, after her morning shower, she went out to get us lattes. A couple of weeks after she left, a package arrived. It was a white ceramic pour-over and two packages of paper filters. A note read: *Buy nice ground coffee. Use the enclosed scoop to put one level scoop of coffee (per cup) in the paper filter. Pour water over top. You will enjoy the coffee. X.* The coffee shops have long since closed, so I have used her gift every morning. I have enjoyed the coffee. ∎

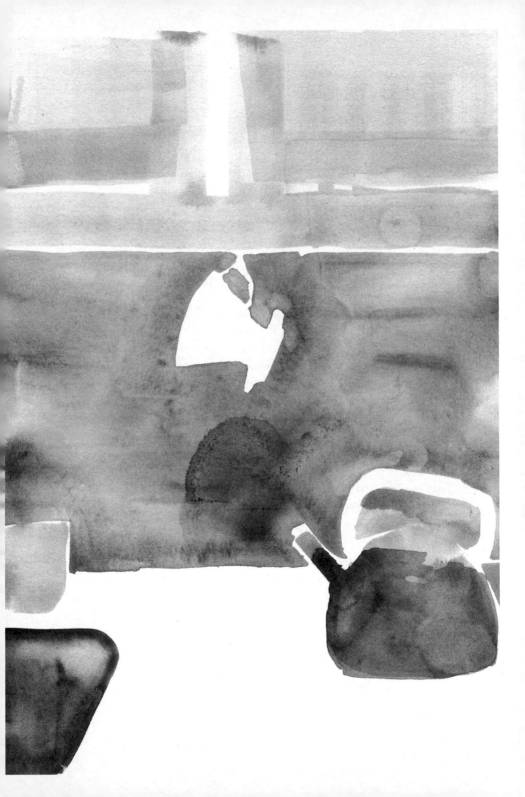

Ken Babstock

Power and Privilege

Not to wet the sand under
your capacity to know your own mind
or point to solar flares
at the appearance of the rainbow ball,
but are you sure you're all right
being in love
with me because I'm not all that functional
or wise or anything?
Closest I've come to watching
Night of the Hunter was reading
an account of Lana Turner pissing
on Robert Mitchum. I've only
just begun banking online. No one
ever includes the freeze response
alongside the other two autonomic
ones. Like biopics of writers,
it's low in action,
drool not being big box office.
I didn't go to school, anywhere,
never mind Stanford.

I think, no, I worry (it's worrying)
you fell in love without

necessarily inspecting
all of these questions. I know I'd be best
served by talking myself somewhere,
like Christoper Robin, somewhere
a friend lived – lives – within their means,
stuck in their own door frame, or expecting
diminishment as more of their lot.
They spent the pages together, didn't they,
obeying the narrative, jumping
in with a quip now and then if the weather
got up, or one of their crew
peeled off into their particular obsessions
giving everyone else something to mull
over. Has Disney bled into
my earliest –? We've all had that nail
through the sole breach the flesh, then
endured the tales of typhus, the dear
old diphtheria, one or the other

going by its street name stood over the draingrate
kicking at the buckling tarmac.
My brother said cocaine can give you lockjaw.
Like the rest of the world's bits,

people either connect or they don't, it isn't
for me to intercede or force the issue,
and look, the chimney pots of Sarajevo
are the city offering the assembled mountains
endless cigarettes at dawn.
I burned ants as a boy. The sun can be narrowed
to a blade. Still, the patriarch
in the Melrose novels
applying the red end of a cigar
made me vomit. It's in the telling, isn't it?
We locate power on a low
stone wall under a fig tree.
We do it all day every day until we can't see.
We do it with a belt between our teeth.
Did you wake to a world vibrating off-key,
sick at the root, pale and untenable?

Jenny Erpenbeck (right) and her mother Doris Kilias, 1999

OPEN BOOKKEEPING

Jenny Erpenbeck

TRANSLATED FROM THE GERMAN BY KURT BEALS

What are you going to do with my furniture when I'm gone? my mother asks me. Oh, I say, we'll see. It's worth a lot, you can sell it. Let's see what happens, I say. You're attached to it, aren't you? I don't say anything. You know we even changed your diaper on the table here. I don't say anything. But it won't fit in your apartment. No, I say.

It's not going to be easy to sell my apartment, my mother says. Don't be silly, I say. The neighbors have been trying to sell theirs for six months and they still haven't managed. Now they want to rent it out. Ah, I say. It doesn't even make sense, it's really nice here. No, I say, it really doesn't make sense. It'll be quite a hassle for you, my mother says. I don't say anything.

My mother says: We have to go to the bank, you need to be authorized to access my account. I know, I know, I say. It's important, she says. Yes, I know, I say. When do you have time – this Thursday? No, I say, I won't be here on Thursday. Next week, then? Yes, I say. When? my mother asks. I tell her I'll have to look at my calendar first. My mother says: Okay. A few weeks later she tells me: I didn't even need your signature, I just had to give them your name.

So when my mother dies, I'm already authorized to access her account. I can use her account to pay for her funeral and the funeral repast, the gravestone and the cemetery fees, I can keep paying off the mortgage and the maintenance fees for her apartment, at least in the short term, while I try to sell it, and I can use a small trust that she left me to cover the monthly rent for the storage unit where I've had her furniture moved.

I choose an urn. I choose a spray of flowers. I choose rose petals to scatter into her grave. I hire a speaker to deliver the speech that I write for my mother. I have her mail forwarded to me. At first the forwarding request can't be processed, because I've forgotten to enter my own name in the 'care of' field. An understandable mistake, since the only reason I'm filling out a forwarding request in the first place is that I'm no longer taking *care of* my mother. I have to submit the form a second time, and this time I write my mother's name, *care of* my name. I cancel my mother's subscription to the daily newspaper that she always read while drinking her afternoon tea, I receive a confirmation that the remaining balance of €202.07 will be refunded. The reason given for the cancellation is: deceased. I send my mother's rail discount card back, the railway company refunds €91.66 of the €110 that my mother had paid two and a half months earlier. I have her telephone service cut off and request that her name be removed from the telephone book. Her final bill, the balance for her last phone calls with me, comes to €16.99. I cancel my mother's account with the radio and television fee collection center. 'This user's account will be terminated at the end of the month. This user's account has no outstanding balance.'

On the morning when my mother is cremated, I spend two hours sitting at home, in front of the window, on the chair where she always sat, waiting for the time to pass.

I cancel my mother's membership to the General German Automobile Association. I write an obituary that appears in the newspaper that she always used to read while drinking her afternoon tea. I receive €170.03 for the obituary.

By the time the tax office inquires what personal property and real property I have inherited – real estate, assets, securities, jewelry, carpets, gold or silver – six weeks have passed since my mother's death. 'All information regarding the value of the estate should reflect the value on the date of death.' But the tax office doesn't want to know if I inherited a half-empty pack of cigarettes, a bathrobe with a used tissue in the pocket, or a bouquet that wasn't even wilted yet. They also don't want to know if I inherited my shoe size, my voice, or the way that I bend over when I put on stockings from my mother. They most certainly don't want to know if I inherited the recipe for meatballs in creamy caper sauce, the straw Christmas tree decorations, or the rummy game with score cards from all the games we played in the past five years, each score written down with the corresponding date. The NS 17 form, which is used to calculate inheritance tax, also doesn't have a column for the 10 bottles of shampoo and 10 tubes of conditioner that I inherited from my mother. My mother bought them all at once in order to get as many golden customer appreciation tokens as possible from the pharmacy and give them to my son, her grandson, to play with. I wash and rinse my hair with that shampoo and conditioner for the next year and a half.

Eight weeks after my mother's death, the artists' social security fund sends me a bill for €1.42 for the last day that my mother was alive, since it was the first (and for my mother also the last) day of the month, but none of the employees of the artists' social security fund would want to know that on that day I took the wet trousers and the wet shirt that the surgeon had cut off of my mother and hung them out to dry on my laundry line, and that I also inherited this way of hanging out laundry from my mother. 'The remaining balance is too low to be automatically deducted from your mother's account. Therefore we ask that you transfer this amount to one of the accounts listed below. Please include your mother's insurance number with your payment.'

I find a stonecutter who makes very nice gravestones and give him the dates of my mother's birth and death so that he can create a design.

And so I inherit a furnished two-bedroom apartment with

108 square feet of storage space in the basement. I inherit bookcases full of books, cabinets with drawers full of files, photos and notes, I inherit a storage closet full of bedding, cleaning products, tools, shoes, large pots, an ironing board, a laundry-drying rack, a broom and a scrub brush, I inherit combs, brushes, makeup, shower gel and creams, inherit dishes, knives and forks, bottle openers, inhalers, aspirin, flower vases, paper clips, diskettes, envelopes, I inherit 1 television, 10 stools, 3 tables, 1 bed, 2 sofas, 2 armoires, 1 cabinet, 1 wardrobe, 11 lamps, 1 chandelier, 5 rugs, 1 wicker chest, I inherit winter coats, diaries, records, I inherit 8 bottles of wine and 3 of mineral water, inherit 1 music box, inherit necklaces, rings and brooches, inherit frozen roasts and frozen zucchini, 2 cans of lentils, 1 half-stick of butter, 1 lemon, 3 pots of probiotic yogurt, inherit 1 bicycle, 1 lawnmower, 1 washing machine, 1 Biedermeier writing desk, 1 wing chair, 2 paintings, 12 framed pictures, 10 apples and 1 banana, some bread, I inherit pens and white paper, inherit twine, coasters and potholders, inherit coins and banknotes from every country imaginable, cardboard boxes of buttons and yarn, 1 large and 1 small sewing box, I inherit hundreds of slides and 3 projectors, inherit 8 ashtrays, 3 cartons of cigarettes, 1 old cassette recorder, 2 mirrors, I inherit 1 computer, 1 printer, 2 old laptops, 1 old monitor, extension cords and 1 toaster, I inherit 2 houseplants, several bedspreads, wool blankets, pillows, inherit empty suitcases, inherit handbags and slippers, nutcrackers, Christmas lights, Easter bunnies, Christmas stockings, 2 boxes of Blue Onion porcelain, tablecloths, towels, eyeglasses, inherit sweaters, stockings, blouses, underwear, inherit cardigans and neck scarves from my mother. I also inherit my own suitcases full of winter clothes that I always kept in my mother's basement in the summer, and my own baby clothes, as well as a little board that I painted when I was in preschool, 2 boxes of stones that I collected as a child and my small Chinese parasol.

After half a year has passed, people begin to ask: Are you writing anything new? No, I say, not yet.

Six months after my mother's death, I pay the bill that the

insurance company sent for the ambulance that took my mother to die, €30. I cancel the insurance policy for my mother's fifteen-year-old car, and give the car to a friend. I hire a real estate agent to handle the sale of my mother's apartment. The maintenance fees and the mortgage for the apartment come to €750 a month. In order for my mother's apartment to be sold, it has to be empty. I start packing boxes. At home, I sort through my own books to make room for my mother's books, papers and photo albums. That winter, I arrange the first move; two movers bring my mother's desk, a cabinet and a trunk to my apartment. The day of the move is icy, and I'm glad that the men don't slip as they're carrying the heavy furniture.

In January 2009, I learn that the manager of my mother's apartment building has run off with so much money that the electricity and water for the whole complex are about to be shut off. To prevent that from happening, the owners' association votes that all members will make two special payments in addition to the regular maintenance fees, in order to 'ensure liquidity'.

My mother's apartment is very nice, but no one buys it, probably because it's too deep in the east side of Berlin, in Weissensee, on the road to Moscow. I send an email to about a hundred friends and acquaintances. No one needs an apartment. I wake up at night haunted by fear.

I go to the stonecutter's shop to inspect his design.

My mother's tax advisor asks me to prepare my mother's tax returns for the months of 2008 when she was still alive. I take a linen chest and various boxes out to our cabin in the country. When I've packed my mother's books, some of the boxes go to my apartment, some go to the antiquarian bookstore, some go to the country. In my search for potential buyers for my mother's apartment, I put up flyers at an art academy in Weissensee. None of the professors needs an apartment.

People ask me: Are you writing anything new yet?

In the process of closing my mother's bank account, I realize for the first time that she also had liability insurance. Unfortunately, I am informed, the payments that have been deducted from her bank account for the entire time that she was already dead cannot be refunded. That spring, barely a year after my mother's death, I rent a small truck and hire two students. We take 10 boxes, the bicycle, the lawnmower and various kitchen utensils to the country. On the drive out and back, we talk about film. That spring, the electric company, which has been providing electricity to my mother's empty apartment for the past nine months, refunds me €119.81. The apartment still costs €750 a month. I decide that if all else fails, I'll rent it out for now, and I place an ad in the paper. Around that time there's some misunderstanding with the phone company, my phone stops working for weeks, and eventually the internet connection goes out, too. My apartment ad appears in the paper, but the phone number that I provided is out of service. In order to sell some lamps, my mother's bed and her TV console on eBay, I have to sit in an internet cafe. While I'm there, I also send emails to the doctors in all eight departments of the hospital in Weissensee, offering them my mother's apartment. None of the doctors needs an apartment.

When an employee at the bank that gave my mother the loan for her apartment hears that I'm planning to rent it out, she advises me that the bank is a public development bank, which means that I'm not even allowed to rent out the apartment on the open market, that is, I can't charge the normal rent, and I have to receive special permission for each tenant. She advises me to refinance the loan.

I inspect the gravestone. The inscription will be colored in with brown paint.

The next move, early in the summer – this time with a moving company – makes its first drop-off at the storage unit, where I leave 1 sofa, 1 cabinet, 3 shelves, 1 armchair, 2 chairs and some boxes. From the storage unit we proceed to my apartment, where I unload some more boxes, a chest of drawers and some pictures.

I hire a second real estate agent to handle the sale or rental of the apartment. He advises me to clear out the very last items that are still sitting or lying around, at least to move them down to the basement for now. I should also take down the curtains and then have the apartment painted.

You must be working on a new book by now, aren't you?

Since a self-employed writer would never be able to get a loan in Germany these days, I spend time negotiating with my husband's Austrian bank about refinancing the loan before my son's school lets out for the summer. The loan is approved, with my husband as guarantor.

I clean everything out of my mother's freezer and pull the plug out of the outlet. Now, for the first time, the apartment is completely silent. I take the frozen food that my mother cooked, carry it home in a well-insulated bag and stash it in my own freezer.

The gravestone is finished now, it's installed in the cemetery. When she finishes her calculations, my mother's tax adviser tells me that my mother is owed a €5 tax refund. My telephone is working again. The internet is working again. On the day in autumn when I finally clean out my mother's apartment once and for all – clean it so thoroughly that not even a bit of thread or crumpled newspaper remains – on that day, when I take my mother's slippers, the scrub brush, the whisk broom, the dustpan and the toolbox down to the basement, when I carry the ashtray with the last cigarette that my mother ever smoked to my car (later, on the drive back to my apartment, the ashes that my mother tapped into the ashtray will crumble), on that day I run into my mother's neighbors in the hall. When they hear that I'm open to renting out my mother's apartment rather than selling it, they say that they'd be interested. A few weeks later we reach an agreement.

Now I'd like to call my mother. ■

Sam Sax

Poem Written from Inside a Leather Pig Mask

only a blade of light makes it
through the eye-slit to the eye.
inside inside sweat from the living
dances with the dead's tanned
stank. in the leather shop south
of market i run my hands over
the animal heads in back behind
the harnesses & straps while
two men who are now surely dead
perform at pleasure on a screen:
the scene is military, the men are sweet.
alone i palm the pig head & hold it
aloft only to slide it over me:
a grandmother's dress & am
transposed & transpossessed back
inside the cow in its lake
of cows penned close as text
outside some missouri township
all knowing they would die but none
imagining they might be remade
into the perverted image of a different
living animal then worn by a man

wanting to be regarded as livestock.
right now this is the queerest thing
i can imagine: the animal yearning
within the animal within the animal.
child who dreams of growing into
a swan only to wake in terror at a mouth
filled with fcathers. i've never been
lonelier than i am right now. inside
this pig mask made out of a cow.
watching these men break into each
other again & again, two men
who will never die.

© LAURENT CHÈHÉRE
À vendre / For sale, 2012
Courtesy of Persiehl & Heine Gallery, Hamburg

GOLDEN VULTURE

Jason Ockert

The turkey vultures glide on updrafts in the lazy blue sky. They circle counter-clockwise, stirring the afternoon. They're dutifully drawn to decaying flesh. The more putrid the carcass, the more pungent the scent, the more birds in the kettle. When the scavengers decide it's time, whatever rots below will be devoured.

By the boy's count, there are eight turkey vultures but he's really only interested in the one with golden wings. It whirls with the others, loop by loop; easy to spot even at a distance.

Before concluding that the wings were made of gold, Hoyt thought it might be a trick of the light. Sunshine in summertime can be deceptive. He's seen diamonds of dew on blades of grass evaporate and quarters shimmering at the bottom of the community pool turn into gum wads. From his tree fort, he's watched sparks of gold rise from the earth and hover in the branches. Before his childhood brain can right itself those fireflies are worth a fortune.

Hoyt has given the vulture ample opportunity to prove it doesn't exist. The boy recently turned ten, which is an in-between age in terms of make-believe. He hasn't lost all his baby teeth but he has lost faith in the tooth fairy. When a knocking sound startles him awake in the middle of the night he knows it's just the wind. His imaginary friends have been replaced by unimaginative flesh-and-blood boys.

A teacher once said that when you hear a ringing in your ear it means that someone is thinking about you, and although he wishes this was true and that his mother was thinking of him on the few occasions when he's heard a high-pitched tingle, he's not sold on the idea. He doesn't believe in ghosts but he's not ready to dismiss God. Satan seems silly but the boy has sensed demons.

Sometimes Hoyt feels an entity beside him. It's a warm pulse of energy that suddenly descends for no discernable reason. It only appears when the boy blinks, which means that he can never see it. After giving it considerable thought, Hoyt has concluded that the thrumming energy is a version of himself – a *shadow*self – living a heartbeat in the past or else a heartbeat in the future. Sometimes the shadowself is trying to hold him back. Sometimes it tugs him forward. Either way, he has no idea what it wants. He wonders if he is a shadowself to a different blinking Hoyt living in another dimension. Maybe that other Hoyt wonders what the here-and-now Hoyt wants, too.

Hoyt spotted the bird through binoculars from his tree fort in the woods behind his house shortly after he'd scarfed down a bologna sandwich. It was early June, when the whippoorwills trill and ants stretch the ground into wavering segmented lines. After determining that the wings were real, Hoyt concocted his plan. He fetched his slingshot, a pillowcase and some duct tape. Now all he has to do is track it down, shoot it from the sky, wrap its beak, carry it home and cram it into Grainger's dog carrier. The dead dog don't need it no more. After that, he'll pull out feathers and grow into a rich, rich man.

The boy begins his adventure tired but in high spirits. He moves quickly with his unusual gait. Hoyt lopes. Always has. Instead of swinging arms, pumping legs and holding his head high, the boy keeps his spine straight, shoulders hunched, elbows pinned to his side and head down. He takes two-step strides. He's learned to walk this way by treading on every other crosstie between the rails.

There is no train anymore. Hasn't been for as long as the boy remembers. The tracks are a quarter-mile behind his modest house in his quiet neighborhood. 'Used to not be so quiet,' says Dad. Dad works the graveyard shift with the road crew on the interstate and sleeps through days. Back then, even without the big racket, there was always the anticipation of sound, his father explained. 'I still hear it echoing in my skull from time to time. The damned trains woke the dog who woke you and once you started wailing there was no stopping it. The racket drove your mother up a wall. Then out the door.'

Hoyt has no memory of being a screaming baby nor does he recollect when his mother left. The last time he asked his dad why she left he said, 'We already discussed this.' The previous time Hoyt had asked why his mother left – as Hoyt recalls – his dad had said the same thing – 'We already discussed this' – so now the boy is convinced that they must have discussed why she left even though he has no memory of that discussion and cannot, for the life of him, pinpoint the reason for the leaving. That might have been an instance when he was rapidly blinking and his father confused him for his shadowself. If the shadowself knows the reason Mom disappeared the boy hopes that he'll figure out a way to share it with him soon.

The only evidence of a train and a mother is a photograph Hoyt keeps in his sock drawer. In the shot, his five-year-old self is hoisting an ice-cream sundae so big it covers the lower half of his face. His mother has a cherry – the one she plucked from his sundae – perched between her lips and she is laughing. Laughing, Hoyt guesses, at something funny Mr Loco just said.

Back when there were trains, there was an ice-cream boxcar called Locomotive's. The owner referred to himself as Mr Loco. He wore a multicolored conductor's hat and handed out complimentary plastic toy-whistle cabooses. When the train ground to a halt, he'd throw open a window, crank up his catchy ditty – 'Go *Cra*-zy for Ice Cream cuz Ice Cream's *Cra*-zy for you!' – and the wide-eyed kids who lived along the tracks would scuttle out of their ramshackle houses with their sweat-stained clothes and ill-fitting shoes and gobble up those sweet treats. Once the passengers were all aboard Mr Loco was off to the next stop. The sticky-mouthed children slouched back to where they were from.

The few stories Dad has told Hoyt about Mom always feature her as sad. Down, out, fidgety. Couldn't keep her hands still, he said. In the picture, though, she seems as happy as anyone Hoyt has seen. She's purposefully crossing her eyes. Clowning around. Her thin wrists are turned upwards, hands bent at odd angles, frozen in some goofy dance. There's a strand of her hair dipping into Hoyt's hot fudge.

You can't see Mr Loco in the photograph but the boy knows he's there because of one hairy hand hovering near Mom's neck. Against her alabaster skin his sharp fingernails are dirty and long. In the shot, Mr Loco appears to be reaching for Mom's throat.

That picture was taken a half-lifetime ago. Shortly after, Mom left and the trains quit.

Railroad weeds slope up the embankment and shoot out of the gravelly soil between the ties. The track resembles the exposed spine of a dormant rust dragon waiting to awaken and rise from the earth. The boy used to hope that he'd be there when the dragon awoke so he could clutch its neck and flap off to some rusty, remote island. He'd have his cool pet smote anyone that got in his way. Then Hoyt felt guilty for imagining a better pet while Grainger, with his hip dysplasia and incontinence, still wagged his patchy tail and cast half-lidded, rheumy, optimistic eyes up at the boy every time Hoyt hurried outside.

So, no dragons. No pets. The golden-winged turkey vulture is a business acquisition. To maintain a sense of distance from it, he's not even going to give it a name. Leprechauns and genies are never given names, after all. Wishers don't want to get too emotional with their prize givers or else they'll start feeling rotten about their wishes.

Just because there aren't trains doesn't mean there isn't danger along the rail. Dad's given Hoyt exploration boundaries. He's allowed to traipse as far north as the water tower and south to Miller's Gorge. Under no circumstance is he allowed onto the railway bridge. Last summer, while father and son were doing dishes in the kitchen and watching the sun set, Dad gave two reasons why Hoyt was forbidden to cross that bridge. Dad, in fact, often gives two reasons. He has offered two reasons why you shouldn't leave the front door open (you let the air conditioning escape and flies come in). There are two reasons that you make your bed every morning (to keep your room presentable in case of a visitor and because it's better to fall asleep when the sheets are tight.) If he can't think of a mate for a single reason he'll say, 'And also, because I said so.'

The first reason Dad offered for not crossing the bridge is that Hoyt might slip and fall to his death in the rocky ravine below. A half-dozen times a year folks die this way. (And though Dad didn't mention it, Hoyt's heard the rumors – and seen the infamous railroad plank spray-painted a faded red – that some really sad people hang themselves from that hunk of wood.) The second reason Dad gave is that Burch is bad news. Burch used to be a coal-producing company town that had a school, library, bowling alley, shopping mall and a roller-skating rink. Then many of the miners got black lung and sued the company before dying. The lawyers made a killing. The company went belly up. Now Burch is Burch in name only. Those who could afford to scurry away did. Everyone else stayed and waited for a coalman with a conscience to roll into town and make the mines operational and safe. 'Fat chance of that,' Dad said, drying a milk glass with a dish towel. 'Only a fool believes in miracles. What's worse is when a fool quits believing. Then he becomes desperate. And desperate folks,' Dad said with a moist hand on his boy's shoulder, 'are dangerous. So stay out of Burch.'

L ast summer, the boy still believed in miracles. That's why he disobeyed his father and crossed the bridge. He wondered, back then, if his mother might be over there. (He did not wonder, for long, if his mother noosed her neck and did the flop, twitch and dangle over the ravine hitched to the suicide tie.) For one full week Hoyt loped over to Burch and searched for her. He started out with high hopes. One time Grainger ran away and the boy found him limping along a fence line near Shotts' farm. The dog had been bitten by some kind of venomous snake – maybe a rattler – and gotten disoriented. The tough mutt survived the ordeal but was never really the same afterwards. Last summer Hoyt hoped he'd find his mother too, with or without a snakebite. If need be, the boy would carry her back in his arms the same way he did with Grainger. In Burch, Hoyt visited the few remaining shops in the ruined mall, he went to the barber shop, he loitered outside three different bars; places where he felt sorrow ooze out every time the front door opened. At the end of that week last summer, Hoyt had learned three things: 1) Neither crossing a railway bridge nor the ruined town of Burch was really dangerous. 2) Mom wasn't there. 3) Miracles schmiracles.

If he knew, Dad would say that hunting a golden-winged turkey vulture is dumb and dangerous. But Dad doesn't know. He's slumbering at home and won't wake for hours. Ordinarily Hoyt doesn't hear his dad return around four. This morning, his father slammed the front door and startled the boy awake. He wasn't able to fall back asleep. Eating breakfast this morning at the kitchen counter, Hoyt decided that he was going to take a nap in the tree house later. That was before he saw the golden-winged bird. There's no time for napping now. The day is bright. Summer break yawns across the calendar.

The boy carries the pillowcase over his shoulder, Santa Claus style. Inside with the duct tape are a dozen donut-hole-sized rocks he's gathered from the creek bed. The frame of the slingshot is made of steel with surgical tubing attached to the uprights. The pocket is made of genuine leather. Closing one eye, slowing his breathing and drawing the sling back to the tip of his nose, Hoyt can smash a bottle from twenty yards away, easy. The weapon was a recent birthday gift from his grandfather – his mother's father – who sent it all the way from Alaska. After the photo of his mom, the slingshot is his prized possession.

As he lopes, the boy alternates from checking the sky to make sure that the vulture is still circling and looking down to keep from tripping. Soon he's at the bridge, then upon it. The water below is brown. The faded-red tie is about midway and Hoyt steps over it. The clouds are too high and strung out to resemble anything. The warm wind blows through the ravine and it does not cool the boy. Soon, he's across.

Once Hoyt's on the other side, in Burch, he approaches the dozen or so company homes built nearly atop the tracks. The houses here are tall and thin and resemble half-gallon cartons of chocolate milk stacked side by side. In the heyday, workers would sit on their tiny back porches eating ice-cream cones as they waited for the coal train. The men who used to live here were not miners. Their job was to haul the trucks from the mines to the tracks and load the coal into the cars. In between they just had to wait. Last summer Hoyt knocked on every door and inquired about his mom to the few suspicious occupants who opened up. Nobody knew anything. Hoyt has learned that nobody ever knows anything, really. Not about his mom, not about where all the trains went, not about coal in lungs and death to dogs. The best part of knowing that nobody knows anything is that you don't have to feel bad when you don't know something either. Like why some vultures are made out of gold.

Beyond the dilapidated homes is a three-story apartment building. It's a place Hoyt never bothered to visit. Each unit has a small balcony enclosed by a metal rail and the facade resembles a set of teeth with braces in bad need of a good brushing. Plastic bags and styrofoam food cartons litter the unkempt, balding hedges a landscaper once planted in a half-hearted effort to provide privacy from the railroad. In the bright sunlight the imperfections are glaring. Hoyt has to squint to see clearly. Overhead, in the tangle of scavengers, the bird with golden wings soars above the rooftop.

Clinging to the side of the building is a fire escape zigzagging to the third floor. Though the boy could easily climb two steps at once, he crouches low and slinks slowly. Just because the birds are attracted to death doesn't mean they don't fear it. He may only get one shot at this. If his aim is true, his life will change forever. His father can quit work and they can build a fortress. He'll teach Dad how to play video games. They'll horse around in the pool with the waterslide and eat ice cream from bowls made out of cookies. He'll buy a bright-blue train and hire someone to paint all of the railroad ties a rainbow pattern and he'll sit in the caboose and throw candy to the awe-stricken children lining the tracks and cotton candy will puff out of the steam pipe and make the air taste super sweet.

When the boy's halfway up the rickety staircase he catches a thick whiff of rot. With every step, the stench grows and by the time he's at the top he's worn out and his unblinking eyes are wide. The neck of the pillowcase is wet with sweat where he clutches it. There, on the stained concrete balcony floor, is a large, oval-shaped platter heaped with a pile of dead rats. Bright white teeth gleam in the sunlight. The long, slender tails drape over the lip of the plate. When the hovering pulse of black flies land upon the mess, wiry whiskers quiver.

A sudden shift in the breeze blows the putrid scent full over the boy and he turns his entire body away to shield himself. He staves off a rising gag and dips his mouth and nose into his shirtfront.

Then Hoyt hears someone say, 'Hello?' and he realizes that he's not alone. There's a partially open sliding glass door that leads from the balcony into the apartment. Against the glare of the glass it's impossible for him to see inside. What he can see is his reflection and he's embarrassed by it. Here is a cowering boy with his face tucked into his sweat-drenched shirt, a heartbeat away from fleeing. That's not how he imagined he'd look when he started out on this adventure. Before he has time to remake himself, the glass door slides fully open and in its place is a thin woman in a hooded sweatshirt and loose jeans. Her dark hair is shocked in streaks of gray and it shoots out from her head in a wild revolt. The woman's face is aggravated by red splotches, as if she were mindlessly rubbing fingertips against her forehead, temples and jaw. Her eyes are all pupils; two black holes sucking in cavernous cheekbones. When she opens her mouth to speak her dry lips reluctantly part.

'I was expecting you around front,' she says.

Hoyt slides his shirt down so the woman can see his face clearly. He wants to show her that he isn't who she thinks he is.

The woman's expression doesn't change. 'Come on in,' she says before disappearing inside.

If Dad were here he'd have more than two reasons why Hoyt shouldn't follow the woman into the apartment. Surely it's a trap. She probably poisoned the rats in order to poison the golden-winged vulture. A woman like that might try to poison him, too. It was foolish of the boy to think that he was the only one who had spotted it. Of course she would expect company. For all he knows, more prospectors are on their way. He'll have to proceed with caution.

It takes a few moments to blink out the daylight so Hoyt's eyes can adjust to the darkness inside. The space is small. There's a wooden coffee table in front of a sagging couch. On the table are a pack of cigarettes, a lighter and an ashtray. A rocking chair is positioned across from the couch. In the tiny dining room, beneath a crooked light dangling from a brass chain, is an enormous harp. A stool sits beside it. The harpist, Hoyt presumes, is in the kitchen standing at the counter, watching the boy.

'Close the slider,' she says. 'I can't afford to air-condition the outside.'

As far as Hoyt can tell, they are alone. The glass door slides smoothly shut.

'What took you so long?' the woman asks.

Hoyt sets his pillowcase on the table and stands next to it. In one fluid motion the boy could brandish the slingshot and defend himself if things go sideways. 'I came as soon as I could.'

'You're pretty young to be a runner.'

'I'm plenty old,' Hoyt says, standing as tall as he can, 'and I didn't run.'

'All right,' the harpist says. 'I'm no one to judge. You are perspiring.'

'It's hot.'

'I'll get you water. Feel free to sit down.'

Hoyt shifts his weight onto his heels and crosses his arms. One thing he's learned from school is that you shouldn't do what a teacher tells you to do right away or else she'll think she can bully you into taking tests and doing homework. If he sits when she says sit, he's her pet. He'll sit if and when it pleases him. Stealing a quick peek outside, he finds that the birds are still overhead. 'I guess your plan is poison. That's not what I had in mind.'

The harpist turns the faucet on and murky water pours into a green coffee mug. 'What?' she says.

'I was just going to stun it and pluck feathers one by one as needed. If you kill it, you cut off the supply.'

Turning the faucet off, the harpist holds the mug in her hand and frowns. 'I'm not following you.'

'The golden-winged vulture. Outside.' The boy juts his chin at the slider.

The harpist isn't wearing shoes. Hoyt notices this as she crosses from the kitchen tile onto the stained carpet in the living room to stand by his side. 'There's somebody out there? Were you followed?'

'No,' Hoyt says, his voice cracking. 'I'm talking about the golden-winged vulture.'

'The what? Golden vulture?'

'Up there. With the others.' Hoyt points.

The harpist follows the boy's finger. Her thin face remains puzzled. 'Yeah, I see them. They're the signal.'

'What signal?'

'The signal that notifies Mr Loco. Tells him I'm ready for a delivery. Those are his rules, not mine. I didn't order Golden Vulture.'

'Who did you just say?'

'Mr Loco,' the harpist replies. Barefoot, she's two inches taller than the boy. 'You do work for him, right?'

Hoyt keeps his mouth shut and tries to work through the confusion. Either the woman has terrible breath or else he can smell the rot from the rats outside seeping in through the slider. The apartment seems to be getting cloudy. There's a vein as small as a thread twitching against the papery skin beneath the harpist's right eye.

'So you don't work for him?'

'No.'

'You saw the birds and came on your own?'

'I came for the golden vulture. You and I can work out a deal but I'm not sharing with anyone else.'

For a moment, the two stand in silence, studying one another. The boy wants to ask about Mr Loco so badly that he can't bring himself to do so. The man might know where his mother is. Hoyt had no idea that Mr Loco was still in business and that he delivered his ice cream. Of course, it makes sense. People might not need coal anymore but they still need dessert.

'I think I will sit down,' Hoyt says. He slumps onto the couch and places his hands in his lap.

The harpist, still clutching the mug of water, shifts her dark eyes from the boy to the bag on the coffee table. 'Golden Vulture?' she repeats.

'Yeah. I guess Mr Loco knows about it.'

'If he does, he didn't mention it to me.'

'Well, it's here now.'

'I see,' the harpist says, folding her arms. She holds the coffee mug crooked. A trickle of water spills onto her sleeve. 'What does Golden Vulture do?'

'It changes our lives.'

'How much does it cost?'

'It doesn't cost anything. It pays us if we can get it.'

'I see,' the harpist says again and when she says this Hoyt knows that she actually doesn't see. People only repeat themselves when they're uncertain of something. Also, the boy can tell that the harpist is scheming. Her eyebrows are bunched together, her lips are slanted into a false smile, and she is breathing out of her mouth. This is exactly the same expression the boy adopts when he's scheming. If his mind wasn't so full he might be able to draw the comparison by glancing at his reflection in the sliding-glass door. Neither boy nor harpist notices the similarities. In both heads wheels turn. Gears grind.

Hoyt's *old* plan was to capture the vulture and live like a king. Actually, the old-old plan – the reason he visited Burch last year – was to track down his mom. Though Hoyt doesn't believe in fate, it is a strange coincidence that the golden-winged vulture led him to the harpist who ordered ice cream from Mr Loco who used to know his mother. That's a fact. The proof is in the photograph.

'You know,' the harpist says, breaking them both out of the daydream, 'I might have some doughnuts in the pantry. Do you like doughnuts?'

'What kind?'

'Glazed.'

'Glazed are my favorite.'

The harpist returns to the kitchen. She pulls a box of doughnuts from the pantry and arranges them on a plate. 'I'm going to make you some lemonade,' she says. For a moment she disappears beneath the sink. When she stands back up, she pours a white powder out of a Tupperware container into the mug. Withdrawing a teaspoon, she stirs the drink slowly. Then she gathers the items and moves into the living room. She sets the plate on the coffee table and the mug and spoon beside the lighter. Up close the boy can see that her fingernails are ragged; bitten down to jagged and inflamed slivers. Her hands are trembling as if she is trying to control a rising fear or else escalating excitement. 'Help yourself.'

Probably, the boy decides, the food isn't poisoned. He just saw her take the doughnuts out of the pantry. Besides, the harpist isn't threatening. Also, he's suddenly ravenous. Lunch was eons ago. He snatches a doughnut, takes a big bite, and chews with his mouth open – a habit his father has failed to break. 'Do you play?' the boy mumbles.

'Not well anymore.'

A familiar faraway sadness creeps into the harpist's wet eyes. He says, 'I'm sure that's not true. I bet you're real good.'

'I used to be decent. I was in an orchestra.'

'Why'd you quit?'

'I didn't. I was cut.'

'How come?'

'I slipped on a patch of ice and snapped my wrist. Just like that, my dreams ended. The bone healed funny. Look,' she says, holding up her arm. 'See how crooked?'

'Yeah.'

'A weak wrist means slow fingers. If your fingers don't fly the harp will chomp you up.'

Hoyt swallows down the last of the doughnut. He considers the instrument and says, 'It looks like a mouth. I've never seen one in person before.'

'Some say it resembles a wing.'

'I can see that.'

'Have you ever heard it?'

'I don't think so.'

'You have, you just don't remember. Here,' she says, standing. 'I'll play you something.' She enters the dining room, adjusts the stool, straddles the short end of the instrument and tilts the body of the harp toward her. Her head is on the other side of the strings and it appears as if she is looking at the boy through bars. Or else the other way around; the boy is the one in the cage.

'This is called glissando,' she says, draping her arms around the harp and quickly running her thumbs and fingertips from one end to the other.

Hoyt snags a second doughnut from the plate and reclines into the couch so that he has a better view. 'Cool.'

'I'll play a little bit of *Fantasia*. You'll recognize the tune. It's about a sorcerer's apprentice.' The harpist gently plucks the strings and coaxes out a rhythm. Her body sways while her face remains tight and severe. Her eyes stay locked on Hoyt. Whatever sadness they held is gone. When she speaks the boy cannot see her lips move. Her words rise out of the harp. 'Be sure to wash that down with lemonade.'

Hoyt lifts the mug to his lips. In the dim, bluish afternoon light the liquid looks brown. When he takes a sip, it tastes bitter. 'Are you sure this isn't tea?'

'Tell me about Golden Vulture,' the harpist says. 'How does it make you feel?'

'Excited, of course.'

'Euphoric?'

'Maybe. I don't know what that means.'

'Real good.'

'I think I'll feel real good if I can catch it.' Hoyt gulps the lemonade to see if it tastes more like lemonade the second time around. It doesn't so he drinks more. Then he decides that it's tea, which he doesn't like. He picks another doughnut from the plate.

'Do you recognize the score?'

'The what?'

'The melody.'

'Not really.'

'Try a little harder.'

Hoyt devours the doughnut and listens. Eventually, he says, 'Maybe I have heard it. My mom might have played it when I was younger.' Hoyt sinks further into the couch and props his head on the arm. 'She knows Mr Loco,' Hoyt says. 'He made her laugh.'

'He makes many mothers happy.'

'Do you think he'll be here soon?'

'Close your eyes. Picture the apprentice dressed in his red robes. See him wave his hands. He believes he's in charge of the entire universe. He conducts lightning and thunder. He sends the waves high into the sky.' The harpist moves her fingers like nimble spiders; the song sounds like it's having a panic attack.

Hoyt takes one last big bite and then closes his eyes. 'I remember. He wore a purple hat, didn't he? With stars on it.'

'But he was only dreaming,' she says quietly while slowly strumming the strings. 'No matter how badly he yearns to be a magician, he's only the apprentice.'

Hoyt listens. A gathering blanket of darkness presses down.

After some time has passed, the harpist says, 'Can I ask you something?'

'Sure,' the boy says. The music has stopped, he thinks. Maybe he can still hear it.

'What are you going to do with your fingers?'

'What?'

'Your fingers. They're sticky. From the doughnuts. Why don't you lick them clean?'

'All right,' the boy says, though he doesn't move.

'Maybe,' the harpist says, 'you won't mind if I have a taste.'

The boy's not certain he heard right. He thinks she's asking him to leave her the last doughnut. That is, if there is another doughnut left. He can't remember if he ate them all. It's too much work to open his eyes and check. 'That's fine,' he says.

In the dream, the boy's fingers are cheese. Rats gnaw them down to bone. A wolf knocks, a cauldron bubbles, the hands of a clock stab out his eyes.

Hoyt awakens into crimson light. He surveys the room and very little of what he sees makes sense: his empty pillowcase is crumpled on the floor with its contents – the round rocks he gathered from the creek bed and the unused duct tape – strewn across the coffee table. There's a steak knife next to his ruined slingshot. The harpist has severed the surgical tubing. The teaspoon holds a charred black oval. A small glass vial sits next to a plastic red cap. The plate is empty. The outside rot-stench is more pungent than it was before. The boy's fingertips are red and raw. The harpist slumps in the rocking chair, a syringe at her bare feet. Her sweatshirt sleeves are rolled up. The tubing from his slingshot is draped around her left arm. Her eyes are cast in the general direction of the boy. There's blood on her lips and a thorn in her smile.

'You poisoned me,' Hoyt mutters. 'You ruined my slingshot.' When he sits up, his dizzy body seems to follow a heartbeat behind. 'I missed Mr Loco.' A part of him longs for sleep. A darker part is breaking free.

Without warning, Hoyt snaps. His shadowself accelerates.

In a blink, he's off the couch, snatching the knife, and with quick, methodical precision he repeatedly jabs the blade deeply into the harpist's chest. The wet sucking sound each slash makes is punctuated by a warm blood spray. The sensation feels familiar. It rings a bell. He's done all this before. The reason his mother is gone is because he killed her. Stab, stab, stab, stab, stab.

After a while, the whir stills. The boy's body catches up with the boy. Soon reason returns. Mom's not dead, she's just gone. The shadow scuttles back into the folds of his brain.

Hoyt sits on the couch with his upturned hands on his knees. He's sweating and breathing heavy. The harpist is in the chair making choking noises. She not dead or dying. She's laughing.

'What's so funny?'

'I couldn't figure out why you came. But I see now.' The harpist has turned her wobbly eyes towards the balcony. 'That gold bird. It's all yellow pain,' she says before doubling over in laughter and nearly tumbling out of the rocker.

'Pain?'

'Yellow pain,' she spits out.

Hoyt turns his attention away from her.

On the balcony, the golden-winged vulture is fretting over the rats. Up close, Hoyt can see that its reddish head is the same color as the suicide tie. The hooked beak dips and rends. Its unblinking gray-brown eyes nest in a wrinkled face. The tops of the wings are black. Only the underside – which Hoyt glimpses when the bird flaps its wings to ward away the other vultures – is golden. Although, it's not gold. It's yellow paint.

He locates a truth in the vulture's eyes: a scavenger, descending upon carrion along the side of a freshly painted interstate. With the vulture perched so close, it's easy for Hoyt to imagine its rapturous feasting. He can picture it flailing its wings in order to claim its portion of the kill. He can envision it along the highway shoulder, sloshing in wet paint and slick blood, gorging with abandon while cars whiz close and swiftly by. And now it's here eating poisoned rats with single-minded hunger. The boy can't decide if before him is a stupid beast or a fearless survivor.

Hoyt stands and collects his things. He opens the slider and the vultures scatter. He steps over the remains of the rats, descends the stairs and leaves the sorceress in her hysterical delirium. Outside it's darker than Hoyt expects, later than he realized. He walks toward the tracks and, through the dwindling twilight, heads home. His mother is and isn't in Burch. Hoyt suspects that he is not alone with his shadowself. There may be a vast army of shadowselves shoving and tugging at other people as they blink their way through life.

When he's upon the railway bridge, Hoyt observes a flock of thrushes rising out of the ravine into the cooling air to hunt mosquitoes. Not vultures, not gold. Just birds. It occurs to Hoyt that there are either too many mysteries for the world to possibly contain or else none at all. ∎

TÊTE-À-TÊTE

Diana Matar

In May 2019, I was offered an artist's residency at the National Archaeological Museum in Naples (MANN), which holds an extensive collection of Greek and Roman antiquities. It was supposed to be a time of research and, unlike most residencies, I wasn't required to produce anything. Instead, it was a rare opportunity for contemplation and an uninterrupted period in which to engage with the museum's works.

I had previously visited MANN fourteen years earlier. It was during a trip to Naples to convalesce after spending nine months in bed due to a serious illness. Over the month I spent in the city I got better and visited the museum several times. I can still remember the first time I saw *Venus Callipyge*, a Roman statue of a woman whose upper body is draped in a cloth of delicately carved marble. I was envious of her obvious robust health and I looked at her until I became physically tired; at her head turned back while she gazed down at her strong physique; at the exquisite expression on her face, poised between her slight insecurity and the admiration for her own body. To this day, in my mind, the museum and that Venus are linked to my recovery.

Returning to MANN I was reminded of how strong my body had become in the subsequent years. I was also aware that although I had a deep emotional connection to the museum, there was almost no association between its collection and my work. I had spent the intervening years photographing places, landscapes and buildings where terrible things had occurred, trying to capture the atmosphere where historical acts of violence have taken place. I was tired of death and of focusing my imagination and camera on places without bodies. I wanted to use the residency to push my work in new directions.

Days after I arrived there was a public demonstration in Naples. People gathered in the rain to protest the inhumane treatment of migrants arriving on Italy's shores. The protesters had marched across the city and ended up in Piazza del Gesù Nuova, a square in the historic district where I was staying. Just as the speeches finished the rain, which had been pouring down, became a mist. But people remained, mingling in groups, talking and signing petitions. I could hear Italian, Arabic, African-accented French and English. The diversity of people's faces captured my attention and I started photographing some of them. Most were still under their umbrellas and the proximity between us made for an intimate encounter, but none of the protesters turned away or asked not to be photographed.

I visited the museum every day. Angela, a specialist in Greek vases with a keen interest in photography, would accompany me through the silent galleries on days when the museum was closed, turning on lights if I desired, giving me information if I asked, but generally leaving me to encounter the works quietly on my own. Becoming more intimate with the vast collection, I narrowed my interest to classical faces. I looked at people portrayed in mosaics excavated from Pompeii and heads cast into ancient coins. I studied warriors' expressions, caught during a battle on the famous *Darius Vase* (340–320 BCE), and the half-scratched face of Zeus in the first-century fresco. But mostly I looked at sculptures. I would circle them, stare into their eyes, and after several days I began to photograph them.

Viewing the figures through a camera allowed me to see them more clearly. I was struck by how closely the sculptors must have studied their subjects, employing a kind of looking that demanded such focus and intent that it enabled them to carve a single whisker of a man's beard. I was surprised to see that although the works sometimes aimed to exalt, they often sought to execute a true-to-life likeness. The features and expressions were uncannily contemporary. Some seemed to be mirror images of the people I had seen at the protest in Piazza del Gesù. They revealed that the classical face, often spoken of being an idealized representation, was deeply complex and realistic. It was African, European and Arab; sometimes heroic, but often immersed in a private feeling or thought, as though caught unawares. Through the lens I saw unique psychologies and imperfections: individuals with scars, physical deformities, emotional complexities and vulnerabilities. I saw the man on the street corner, the woman in the shop, the boy who had left his family to cross the sea.

In one of the grand halls, there were several busts of Marcus Aurelius, each by a different artist and crafted many years apart. There were also sculptures of Caesar, Tiberius, Claudius and Hadrian. But it was the modest bust of an unknown boy that interested me most. I looked through my camera and he seemed to be returning my gaze.

Although we look at people all the time, I wonder how often we recognize the distinctiveness of those we encounter? Perhaps taking a portrait is an allegory in seeing the singularity of another person. Portraiture is a unique photographic genre, one that I have had a relationship with for more than two decades, but rarely practice. Over the years, though, I have noticed that when the sitter has an idea of how they want to project themselves, the portrait most often fails, and when I predetermine what I wish to communicate about the subject before meeting them, the photograph usually lacks life and authenticity. A portrait entails an exchange between the photographer and the subject, and that exchange necessitates they see each other clearly. I approached the sculptures in the museum as if they were individuals. And even though they are made of stone, they responded. ■

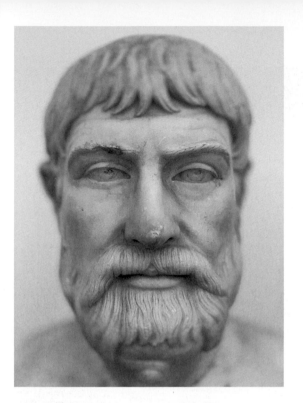

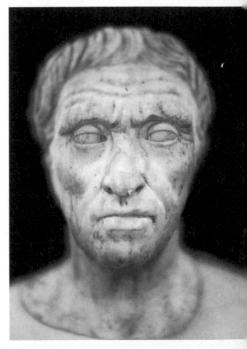

AESTHETICA CREATIVE WRITING AWARD

SUBMIT YOUR WORK

Win £1,000 & Publication
Deadline 31 August 2020
www.aestheticamagazine.com/cwa

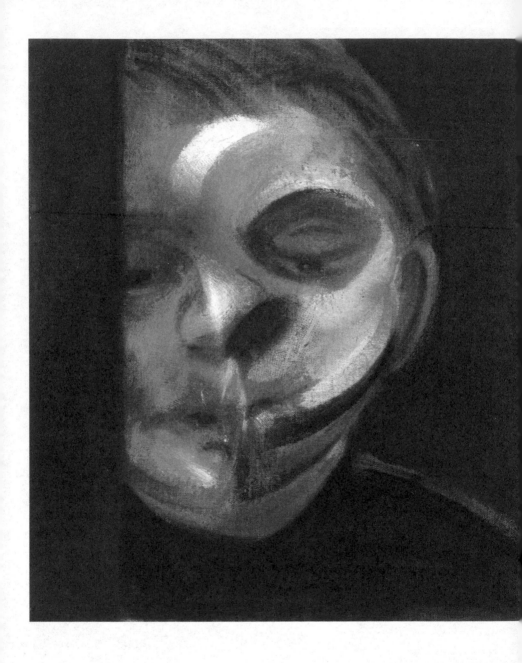

FRANCIS BACON
Self-Portrait, 1972
© The Estate of Francis Bacon. All rights reserved, DACS/Artimage 2020

THE TEMPTATION
OF ST ANTHONY

Mark Haddon

The shattered mosaic floor on the far side of the courtyard wobbled and blurred in the blistering heat. He had woken at dawn and been praying ever since. He had not eaten today nor had he drunk. He would wait until the craving had passed, then allow himself to do both when it became a choice, not a lost battle in his long war against the base needs of the body. There was grit under his knees. The pain was mortality made manifest. It demonstrated the shape and strength of that which he must rise above.

For eighteen years he had lived inside the ruins of this little Roman fort in the desert past Krokodilopolis, devoting himself entirely to worship and contemplation, wearing rags and depending entirely on the charity of nearby villagers for sustenance. The original roof was long gone, but the walls, though partially collapsed in places, were still high enough to hide the surrounding landscape so that he could see nothing beyond the fort but sky. There was little protection from the sun during the day and no protection from the cold at night. The worst of the wind was kept out at least. He stored his food and water in the slim wedges of shade inside the perimeter of the compound and relieved himself in the far corner where scavenging insects consumed his excrement before it was dry.

The devil had tempted him forcefully and relentlessly. A rain of gold coins lay on the ground for days, finally evaporating when he refused to touch them. Every so often a great trestle table of pies and tarts and wines would appear in the centre of the courtyard. The devil himself would sit in his ear for days on end talking softly about all the pleasurable and profitable things he could do with his life. Demonic women had appeared in the small hours and invited him to join them in a range of sexual acts that beggared belief. Angered by his persistent refusal to weaken, the devil had sent a swarm of tiny, blood-red demons with spines like needles and razor teeth who tore his flesh to shreds, leaving his body permanently peppered and striped with scars.

A fat, brown scorpion sidled on to a rock beside him, its tail vibrating. It looked like a real scorpion but it was hard to be certain about such things, and he had to be on his guard. In the corner of his eye he could see a vulture turning overhead. One had landed on him a few months ago, puncturing his left shoulder with its talons and hacking out a chunk of his scalp with its beak. He had flinched and cried out and the bird had flown sullenly away.

The scorpion descended from its rock and scuttled off.

He could hear distant voices, a faint whoop and the slap of leather on powdery stone. He would not turn immediately. He would not allow himself to be steered by mere events. Neither, however, must he be ungracious. Bringing his prayers to a decorous pause, he got slowly to his feet. His knees were like the rusted hinges of an old door. He assumed the villagers were delivering bread and water, and indeed, when he turned, he saw the silhouette of the boy, Jarwal, standing in the notch in the southern wall that must at one time have been a window. But Jarwal was reaching down and hoisting a second person up beside him.

Another ogler come to see the hermit? He had asked that such people be gently dissuaded wherever possible, but some were wealthy, the villagers were poor, and he relied upon their goodwill.

The second silhouette was that of a robed woman, and if she was an ogler then she was a very insistent one because Jarwal was

helping her climb down the slope of tumbled stones to the floor of
the courtyard. He raised his hand intending to shout, 'Stop!' but he
had not talked, let alone cried out, for a very long time and no sound
came from his mouth.

The woman was walking towards him carrying a basket. He did
not want to be in the company of a woman. She was, thank God,
not one of the phantoms who stepped naked from the shadows in
the middle of the night. If the visitor were a man he might have been
carrying news of sufficient weight to justify breaking the intrusion,
but no one would entrust a woman with a task of such import.

She stopped a few paces in front of him and put the basket down.
Ten loaves and three leather bottles of water. 'I gather these are yours.'
The voice was so familiar it could have emanated from inside his own
head. She pushed her hood back and looked around. 'I had heard
that it was austere but I did not expect quite this level of ostentatious
self-flagellation.'

He felt giddy. His sister had become a woman. 'You . . .' He
sounded like a raven. He coughed to clear his throat and tried again.
'You should be in the convent.'

'Don't worry. I'll be going back.'

'As for ostentation . . .' He coughed again.

'I have no money of my own. You gifted the order the little wealth
you did not give away. They are, in consequence, the only people who
will look after me. Unless I can find myself a husband. Which is not
easy from inside a convent.'

He was about to defend himself but she cut him off for a second
time. 'You sold me to nuns.'

'I didn't sell you to anyone.' His sister seemed as unwilling to take
instruction as she had been when she was a child, and the convent
had not improved her. Arguing was pointless.

She sat down on a crumbled pediment, uncorked one of the
goatskins, hoisted it to take a generous swig then tore the end from
one of the loaves. It was hard to tell whether she was genuinely
hungry or whether she was trying to goad him. 'Father indulged you

too much. You grew up thinking that constant praise was normal and that other people were unimportant.'

'I care little for your opinions about me, but you should not speak ill of our father.'

'The nuns are vile, by the way.' She picked a tiny stone from the bread and flicked it away. 'Unsurprisingly, the majority were deposited there by rich families who wanted them out of the way. It has made them very bitter.'

'A life devoted to Christ . . .'

'The ones with vocations are worse. Vinegary little witches. They need our money but they hate our company.'

He took a deep breath. 'Did you come here with some serious purpose?'

'Then Father died and there was no one to revere you. You couldn't sing, you couldn't paint, you couldn't argue fluently. You had fallen off a horse so many times we lost count. You were neither intelligent enough to practise law nor diligent enough to handle other people's money. But you had to be better than everyone else, didn't you.' She looked around scornfully. 'So you picked a challenge too pointless for anyone else to better.'

She looked up at him and he saw that she was crying. 'I could have been happy. I could have been a mother. You threw my life away in return for this.' She hurled the remaining crust across the courtyard where it cartwheeled to a halt and lay in the little cloud of dry dust it had raised.

He was angry that she was so wilfully misinterpreting everything he had done. He was angry that she was dismissing his years of sacrifice as self-indulgence. He was angry most of all that she was able to stir up these violent emotions.

Then he was not angry. He was overwhelmed instead by a memory of standing in a sunlit courtyard. He was fifteen years old, his sister seven or eight. It was spring or autumn, the air neither too cool nor too hot. His mother was weaving on a small handloom, yarns of indigo, turmeric, kermes red. He could hear the splash and slap of the servant girls washing clothes in the trough in the adjacent courtyard. His father was elsewhere in a dark room, poring over diagrams and accounts. His sister sat cross-legged in front of his mother. She had arranged two clay people and a little clay horse on the stone in front of her and was making them act out some ridiculous drama. The sun falling through the quince tree littered the ground in the centre of the courtyard with tiny overlapping circles of brightness like fallen blossom.

Within three years it would be gone, his father left paralysed by a seizure then wasting away over the following months, barely able to eat or drink, his mother dying shortly after from the annual fever which swept through the city in the damp heat of summer.

His sister was right. He had been so consumed by his own grief that he had not considered hers. They had both lost their parents. He had been a young man, but she was still a child. How was it possible to be so blind for so long to such obvious facts?

An uprush of warmth towards his sister was overtaken by his shame at never having felt it before. He walked over and knelt in front her. 'I am profoundly sorry. I treated you very badly indeed. I told myself that everything I did was done to serve the Lord. I should have remembered that serving the Lord means, first and foremost, looking after one's own family.' He felt better for having simply spoken the words out loud.

She stared blankly at him as if he had spoken in a language she did not understand. 'I am forced to sleep on a straw mattress in a room with five other women. One of them has lost her mind and whines constantly like a sick child.'

'You have every right to be angry with me and I am painfully aware of my having no means of recompense for the wrong I have done you.'

He paused. He couldn't say, at first, what caught his attention. Some animal faculty was warning him of danger. He remained perfectly still for a few moments. He could hear his sister breathing, the soft hush of windborne sand moving across stones and, every few seconds, the clang of a goat bell.

Then he smelled it, the faintest trace, the stink he had not smelled since the day some months back when a hyrax died and burst and oozed and dried up in the courtyard, felled by a sickness so vile that even the birds of prey would not touch the corpse. He felt sick in both body and spirit.

'Brother . . . ? Something is wrong.'

He forced himself to ignore the voice of doubt. He had to do this and he had to do it quickly. He stood up, lifted his arm and struck his sister hard across the face so that she was thrown on to the ground by the force of the blow. She lay there not moving for what felt like a very long time indeed, then lifted herself slowly back on to the pediment, the red print of his hand bright on her cheek. 'And this is how the famous holy man behaves to his own sister.'

'You are not my sister.'

He wondered briefly whether he had made the most terrible error, then she let out a long growl and her eyes turned black. Her skin smoked and crackled and split and peeled away like the skin of a rabbit being roasted over an open fire. The same stink but overpowering now. He stepped backwards. She had been transformed into a hairy, snarling ape, spittle flying from her mouth. She sprang on to his chest, knocked him to the ground and fastened her sinewy hands around his neck. 'You doubted. For a few minutes you doubted everything. I came *so* close. Next time I will shatter you completely.'

There was a bang as loud as a house collapsing and the creature exploded, covering him in clumps of brown fur and gobbets of sticky fat bearing the same foul stink, which he had to peel away one by one before washing himself with a mixture of dust and precious water.

He felt wounded over the following weeks in a way that he had not felt wounded before, and it took longer for him to heal. He had been blindsided. He had won the battle but the margin by which he had done so was terrifyingly thin. There were nights when he began to question his vocation, bitterly regretting that he had so thoroughly razed his previous life that now his only choice was between religious poverty or poverty with neither meaning or purpose. Gradually, however, the same lack of choice gave him comfort and encouragement. There was a single path open to him. He did not need to waste time and effort in pointless debates with himself, he need only put one foot in front of the other. So he applied himself to his daily routine with redoubled vigour, he consoled himself that any mental bruises were useful reminders of his all-too-human failings and he gave thanks to God for pointing out his self-centredness.

It had rained sparsely and infrequently during the years of his confinement, but that winter a deluge fell from a night sky rumbling with thunder and cracked by bolts of lightning, turning the entire fort into a pool of freezing water. He knelt in it, praying until his frozen legs were too numb to support him and he was forced to stumble and splash through the absolute dark and take refuge on a fallen column. A burst of blue-white fire revealed, for the briefest moment, two rats sitting beside him, equally sodden and perplexed.

Drying off in the sun the following day he began to see the storm as a divine cleansing, of earth, of body, of soul. While he tried very hard not to make predictions or draw conclusions or, worst of all, congratulate himself, it seemed to mark a turning point in his journey, a summit after which the path became easier and the landscape ahead more clearly visible. There were difficult dreams and days of doubt, but the devil no longer appeared to him in person. He heard no bodiless voices, met with no animals who seemed anything more than creatures seeking shade or taking shelter or trying to steal his bread.

The oglers came in steadily increasing numbers but he accepted their appearances with as good a grace as he could muster, even when some of them refused to leave and put up tents and lean-tos outside the fort. The quiet and the calm he had enjoyed for so long was now interrupted not simply by the wind and bird cries and the bleating of goats but by the faint sounds of human conversation, the slap of canvas, the clink of pans and the clatter of wheels. Occasionally he saw a thin column of smoke rising above the wall and smelt meat being cooked.

When some of these men – for they were all men – came into the compound to ask for guidance he would instruct them to commune in silence with their Maker, to abjure the demands of the body and to live as simply as possible. He would point out, in addition, that they could do these things anywhere. They did not need to be near him, they needed to be near God.

According to Jarwal there were now some sixty or seventy of them camped round about. He could feel their presence even in the silence of the night, the way they pressed against his solitude, the way they made the heavens smaller. He had left the city and gone into the desert to escape everything that might distract his attention from his holy vocation, but the city had finally tracked him down and was in the process of swallowing him up again.

He forced himself to rise above his petty grievance. This piece of land, these ruins, had not been given to him for his sole use. All men stood in the same relation to God and no one had precedence over another. God neither spoke to him alone, nor cared for him alone. These men were not impeding his religious self-betterment, he was impeding theirs. It might seem arrogant to suppose that he had anything to teach these . . . he could think of no word that did not make him feel uncomfortable. Followers? Acolytes? Disciples? But was it not more arrogant for him to refuse to help them?

He came slowly to accept that this phase of his life was over. He had a new calling and the fact that he did not want this calling was of no relevance. He was a servant of the Lord and it was not his place to dictate the tasks he was called on to perform. His distaste for company, for conversation, for noise, for activity, these things were no different from the physical pains he had previously taught himself to overcome in pursuit of a higher purpose. He would grieve for the loss of his solitary life, but he had already put one life behind him entirely, he could do it again.

He took the decision that he would leave the compound shortly after Easter so that he might, for one last time, celebrate Christ's death and rebirth on his own before re-entering the world. He spent the period of Lent fasting, sleeping little and praying constantly, asking God to give him strength and wisdom for the new and challenging task ahead.

He climbed the wall at dawn on Easter Monday, hoping that few of his followers would be awake and that the shock of re-entering the world would not be doubled by the shock of finding himself at the centre of a crowd.

It was not the makeshift village that troubled him most, large as it was – a wide, jumbled moraine of temporary dwellings which ringed the fort entirely – nor Krokodilopolis in the distance, nor the silver slice of the oasis, nor the seemingly endless desert beyond, but the sheer wheeling monstrosity of space which contained these things. He stooped and placed his hands on the dusty stone until the vertigo receded, as one might do travelling in the back of a cart along a rutted road.

Getting to his feet again he saw a man squatting to relieve himself, thawb bunched around his waist. The man looked up and cried out and within moments numberless other men were clambering up and circling him like hunting dogs around a felled quarry. He could not hear what they were saying. He had not listened to people talking over one another since entering the fort. The warm, animal smell of them, the shock of being touched, the vastness of the horizon then this press of bodies. But they were further away now, their voices had become muffled, the sun was dimming as if it were evening and he was falling backwards very slowly.

'He is unwell,' shouted one man. 'Give him space.'

He was hazily aware of being carried into a shady tent and laid on a bed of terrible softness, and while he wanted to protest at a luxury dangerous both to him and to them, he did not have the energy and, in truth, he was relieved to be in a cool, dark space with only two men.

'Drink,' said one, holding a clay cup to his lips. 'Drink.'

He drank and slept and woke some hours later. He insisted that he must not lie in the shade but must be outside praying in the heat of the sun. When he went outside to do so, however, he found himself mobbed. He asked those around him to join him in prayer and some of them did so but the noise and press of those further away, by whom they were surrounded, made quiet contemplation impossible. He tried to call out to these men but his voice had become a small thing over the years and they could not hear him. He felt overwhelmed, as if he were sinking in an ocean of men and were going to drown if he did not climb on to dry land. Eventually he returned to the cool of the tent, exhausted, ashamed and perplexed.

His cravings for stillness, for space, for empty hours, these were simple things to overcome. Over the coming days he was reminded that dealing with other human beings could often be well-nigh impossible. He had forgotten how hard it was to understand what was going on in another man's mind. He had forgotten that one could be on good terms with two men who hated one another. He had forgotten how well people lied, to others and to themselves. He had forgotten their capacity for saying one thing and doing another and being utterly unaware of the contradiction.

He constructed a regimen that would act like a map to get him through the difficult weeks ahead. He slept and ate in the company of different men every night so that none might count themselves as favourites or be counted by others as favourites. He spoke to, and prayed with, small groups in tents so that they might at least be able to hear one another clearly and find some relative peace, and he tried to do this. He tried to be a friend to all and to treat the whole encampment as his home.

He began, gradually, to feel more at ease in company, less disturbed by the noises and smells, the distractions and demands. His voice grew stronger. On a couple of occasions he clambered up on to the wall of the fort and spoke to those gathered below him, and this soon became a weekly, then a daily act.

'Let us not think, as we look at the world, that we have renounced anything of much consequence, for the whole earth is very small compared with heaven.'

He instructed his followers to put aside the eating of meat and the drinking of wine and commit themselves to the simple diet of bread and water that had sustained him for nearly two decades. He instructed them to live without the false comforts of warmth and cleanliness. He instructed them to pray constantly and not waste energy in idle talk among themselves. He instructed them to undertake tasks that would purge the body of sinfulness, to remain still for long periods, to pass nights without sleep and days without food. Some of them submitted to his edicts, some were unable to rise to the challenge and returned to the world, but they were soon replaced by a growing number of others.

He shared with the increasing crowds the story of his own experiences so that it might prove an example. He told the stories of the gold and the pies and the demonic women and the tiny, blood-red demons. He described how Satan had appeared to him in the guise of his sister.

'So let us intensify our discipline against the devil, for a good life and faith in God are great weapons. Christ has given us power to tread upon serpents and scorpions, and upon all the power of the enemy.'

Not all those who left the encampment did so because they found the rigours of this ascetic life too hard to bear. A handful not only embraced his teaching but walked even further out into the emptiness of the desert to find places of solitude where they, in turn, might come closer to their Maker, and it was the news of these men that, more than anything, persuaded him of the rightness of his decision to abandon his solitary life in order to preach.

Spring became summer, summer became winter, winter became spring. He had lived among his followers for nearly a year, by which time he had gathered about him a community of a thousand men or more, all devoted to living a holy life.

As Lent began he was acutely aware of the difference between this year and the last. He still felt a yearning when he recalled his final month in the fort, pushing his body past fatigue, past discomfort, past doubt, past wilfulness into that place of profound stillness which seemed to lie just beyond the borders of the material world. But he had discovered a new and different joy in a vocation shared, the holy power of a community united in a single spiritual aim. Over those four weeks of penance, mortification, repentance and self-denial he felt every man slowly finding his place, like blocks being shaped and fitted by a master mason so that their individual bodies could be used to build a cathedral of souls.

The night before Easter Sunday they all remained awake in prayer, and in that communal silence he felt closer to God than he had ever done in his years of seclusion.

When the first splinter of sun blazed at the desert's far edge he rose and drank a little water and broke a crust of bread with those nearest him. Then he ascended to his usual spot on the ruined wall from which he could be seen by everyone in order to preach from the Gospel according to Mark, which was written, like much of the New Testament, on the pages of his heart.

'Now when the Sabbath was past, Mary Magdalene, Mary the mother of James, and Salome bought spices, that they might come and anoint Him . . .'

It was always his favourite time to preach. His voice seemed to be louder and to reach further, as if the air itself had been rinsed and cleansed by the night of all the sounds it had held during the previous day.

'And they said among themselves, "Who shall roll us away the stone from the door of the sepulchre?" And when they looked, they saw that the stone was rolled away: for it was very great.'

A man with a red beard standing directly below him was laughing. He felt a shiver of irritation but reminded himself that there were those among his followers who were not of sound mind and they should be the object of pity and persuasion, not public correction.

'And entering into the sepulchre, they saw a young man sitting on the right side, clothed in a long white garment; and they were affrighted.'

Several men on either side of the red-bearded man were laughing now. His first thought was to turn round to see if something was happening behind him or nearby which had occasioned such amusement, but the laughter was spreading and there was a tangible malice in it that was very clearly directed at him.

'Be not affrighted,' he said. 'Ye seek Jesus of Nazareth, which was crucified . . .'

Then he smelt it, the hyrax stench, the burst and the ooze of it. A well shaft opened in his bowels. This was surely not possible. A hundred men were laughing now, two hundred, five hundred, a thousand, mouths open, heads thrown back, hands spread theatrically on their aching chests. The smell made him retch. The laughter became a roar. He put his hands over his ears. He could neither speak nor run. A thousand pairs of eyes turned black at the same time.

'No, no, no, no, no . . .' He braced himself. There would be some kind of explosion, there would be fire or flood, the men would be transformed into beetles or rats in order to feast on him, or be gathered together into a single daemonic creature of huge proportions.

None of these things happened. The roar began to soften and diminish. The men themselves seemed less substantial, more like pictures of men painted on the air, then coloured mist, then nothing. There was silence.

The sun was fully risen now. He looked around. There were no tents, there were no fire circles, no latrine trenches, no footsteps in the sand, no cart tracks. Everything was exactly as it had been when he entered the compound twenty years before.

'*Pater noster qui es in caelis,*' he recited quietly, '*sanctificetur nomen tuum, adveniat regnum tuum* . . .' But the words were nothing more than sounds coming out of his mouth, as empty as the call of a bird or the bleat of a goat. The whole of the last year had been an illusion. He had thought himself worthy of a thousand followers. The work of his entire life had been rendered worthless by his own vanity. He began to sob. He had not sobbed since he was a small child. He wanted his long-dead mother to pick him up and put her arms around him and he was terrified by the force of this need and the clarity of the memory.

He was getting to his feet. He had not taken a decision to get to his feet. He was walking along the top of the wall, powerless to stop himself. He had always been powerless to stop himself, that was the truth. He was merely sitting astride the beast of the body as it followed its own base path. Will was an illusion. Control was an illusion. Perhaps God himself was an illusion.

He was standing at the highest corner of the wall now, below him a field of jagged stones as rough as ploughed earth. He looked into the smoky distance. No habitation, no trees, no animals. Two tiny dust devils made their slow progress over the plain. The great, unpeopled stillness that had previously been a great church was now a howling void. He stepped forward so that his naked toes curled over the edge of the wall. If his head struck the rocks first then he might at least be granted a swift passage to whatever world lay beyond this one. Was it hell that awaited him? He knew only that no hell could be more painful than this existence. He leant forward and fell into the empty air like a man falling on to a bed at the end of a hard day's work.

He was not dead. That much was clear. He was in a great deal of pain and someone, or something, was licking his face. He opened his eyes. The something was a stray dog. He pushed it away then wiped his forehead and found it covered in a sticky paste of blood and dust. The dog cocked its head to one side, examining him. It was a scrawny creature, its fur a dirty, sun-bleached yellow, like pretty much everything else in the landscape.

He forced himself to sit up. For a few moments he had no idea of how he had got there. When the memory returned it was like someone cutting open his abdomen, reaching in and hauling his guts out through the wound. He felt sick and faint. He could not blame the devil. The devil had merely opened a door through which he had confidently walked.

He thought briefly about standing up but he could see no reason for making the effort. There was nothing he had to do, no one to whom he could turn, not even God himself. He had crowned his failings by trying to throw away the most precious of all gifts. '. . . and he that shall blaspheme against the Holy Ghost hath never forgiveness, but is in danger of eternal damnation.'

The dog had a single patch of grubby white fur across its chest and down one leg.

He was painfully hungry and desperately thirsty. He had been painfully hungry and desperately thirsty for twenty years.

He lay for a long time looking up into the relentless blue sky. How long would it take for him to die if he did not move. Days? Weeks? Then he remembered that one of the villagers, Jarwal perhaps, would be along sooner or later. He did not want this to happen. If others knew what he had done it would only magnify his shame. He had to leave this place.

He got carefully to his feet. The world spun and slowed and came eventually to a standstill. He had to go somewhere but he had no idea where. Perhaps he should simply walk further into the desert and let the buzzards pick his bones clean.

The dog was still there. It lifted a leg and scratched vigorously behind one ear. He liked the dog's company. The dog did not judge him. They were both outcasts.

Was it a real dog? He had no strength left to worry about such things.

He remembered the devil visiting him in the body of his sister. The vision of the courtyard, the light under the quince tree, the sound of the servants washing, indigo and turmeric, the little clay figures his sister was playing with. That uprush of warmth. He wished he had listened to the stories she told herself.

He wanted to see his sister again. He was surprised by the clarity of this thought and the strength of the feelings it stirred up. Was she still alive? The possibility of her having died made him feel panicky and lost.

He calmed himself. If he needed an answer to the question then he could find an answer. It would be a journey of several weeks even if he had money, but it was possible. He had little else to do.

He looked at the dog, half expecting some kind of agreement, but the dog was lying down in a little strip of shade, oblivious to his dilemma.

And if his sister was alive? If he found her? His welcome might be a very cold one. It did not matter. At the very least he could apologise for what he had done all those years ago, then turn and walk away. He would have tried at least. He would have settled some small account.

He would start by heading to Krokodilopolis. He would beg for money and use it to buy a place in one of the caravans. If no one gave him money he would work for it. If he had learnt one thing over the last twenty years it was how to put up with discomfort and live frugally.

'Let's go.' He said it without thinking.

The dog got lazily to its feet.

He began walking and the dog fell into step beside him. ∎

I am about to be ticketed for my poor handwriting. An intimidating soldier walks over and asks to see my note. 'You should avoid using grid paper,' he admonishes me. 'What is your stated reason for leaving your apartment?'

It is a desire to emerge from the depths of withdrawal, I would like to tell him, to escape my growing interiority and to find an implausible freedom from this lockdown. But I offer a more conciliatory response, mostly because he carries a truncheon.

'To get some exercise and fresh air,' I offer. 'The law says that we're allowed to go out for an hour.'

'That's not what you're doing,' he replies. 'Your stated purpose is exercise, but you're sitting on a bench reading, and don't write on grid paper next time.'

It is true that I am sitting on a bench reading while our children ride their scooters and my wife climbs up the austere limestone steps of the Cascade. Fernando Botero's giant bronze cat looms over me, with its black tongue sticking out. A stray dog barks in the distance. Ever since the pandemic, our neighborhood is mostly deserted, except for the pigeons and statues.

'What are you reading, anyway?' the soldier asks.

'It's a novel by Claude McKay,' I say. A book set in Marseille, my escape to the outside. Reading it, I pretend to see the horizon, the sea beyond our closed borders, that unanchored freedom.

The soldier shrugs. Maybe he smiles, I can't tell with his medical mask on. ∎

1. The White City

In the summer of 1999, during the post-war period in Serbia following the NATO bombing, I spent a few contented months in Belgrade.

I say 'contented' because the four miserable wars that had haunted that broken country were drawing to a close after so much hatred, so much misery, so much violence.

I felt somehow rejuvenated: I had found a group of young friends, all Serbs, who distracted me from my work and, more importantly, from myself.

Belgrade was a new experience for me. I had spent the Bosnian conflict on the other side of war – besieged Sarajevo, largely with Bosnian Muslims and Croats. I was never given a visa to what was referred to – in an ungainly way – as 'rump Yugoslavia'.

Denied access to Belgrade, I had fantasies of the White City, as it is known. In Sarajevo, which was deprived and dangerous, we imagined Serbs existing with things we painfully lacked: water, heating, access to food. The Serbs did have those commodities, but they were suffering their own existential exile, as well as sanctions; and worse, innocent people who had nothing to do with politics or war, were being treated as international pariahs.

The Yugoslav wars began in Slovenia in 1991 and ended in June 1999 in Kosovo. That summer, I felt a heaviness lifting. Restrictions were easing. I installed myself in the nearly empty Hyatt Hotel, an ugly building overlooking public housing on one side, but with a view of the Sava River on the other.

I was there for the long haul, armed with a map, an address book and a few airy summer dresses I had picked up in a flea market before the NATO bombing started in March. I had a driver who was also a part-time martial artist. I began exploring an entirely different former Yugoslavia, not the wartime Bosnia I had known. I met with war criminals, mafia bosses, sanction busters, small-time thieves: men who stole truckloads of La Perla lingerie at gunpoint in Italy and drove them across the borders to Serbia.

I met with spirited young revolutionaries who, the following year, would overthrow the government and get rid of Slobodan Milošević for good. I met spiritual healers and country people, relatives of Milošević, gymnasts and karate instructors, musicians and actors. All of them were coming out of a long, dark hibernation.

I was used to life during wartime, but it was really my first post-war experience. In both cases, life seemed frozen. I remember entire winter months passing while I was living in Sarajevo being unaware of the date or even the day of the week. One day would merge into the next: rise, do some jumping jacks to get warm, find something to eat, find some water to wash. Work. Sleep dreamlessly. Fear forces you to live in the present. In war, there is no future and there is no past.

Belgrade, post-war, had a similar rhythm. Most shops were still closed. So were museums, universities and clubs. My new friends, in their early twenties, were a lost generation, coming of age during war. Their lives were halted in time, a predicament they accepted with grace, sometimes even with humor.

They appeared to be floating. Their university degrees were suspended because classes had been stopped. Some of them with specific interests in subjects such as archaeology weren't allowed to travel to sites that were now in the hands of the military.

Others, studying art history, could not go to the Louvre or the Prado or the Uffizi. Even if there were international flights, they could not get visas to enter France or Spain or Italy.

That summer, I began to understand this concept of time. The seasons were changing – the wet April and muddy May when NATO led the bombardment against Serbian targets shifted into a humid, luminous June. The trees in Kalemegdan Fortress, where you could see the Sava and Danube Rivers meet, were verdant and lush. Nature was moving ahead, even if my friends were not.

Still, we made merry. We went to coffee bars and picnics and drank much Montenegrin wine; we went to parties in dusty apartments with portraits of the Serb royal family pre-World War I.

People did not discuss their time of war, their confinement. 'We have lived through enough,' my friend Ivana told me. 'I don't have much more to say.'

I also remember the heavy sorrow I felt in Belgrade those months, as I walked down the empty Knez Mihailova, past the French Cultural Center windows smashed by angry Serbs when French jets bombed their positions. My many years in Yugoslavia have left me with an indelible streak of nostalgia. Days, months, years – time I wished to be over because I was uncomfortable – could never be restored.

Even now, if I am in Europe in November and see a flock of storks passing overhead, I am transported back to wartime Croatia and hear the voice of a friend telling me how birds migrate from the Balkans to Africa, sometimes traveling for days without stopping. I remember the yellow field we were standing in; the color of a muted gray sky.

I remember being halted in a car in a snowstorm in the Krajina for hours. We were stuck in a snowdrift, the car would not budge, night was falling, temperatures were dropping. Suddenly, an ancient man, dressed in a World War II uniform, silently let himself into our car. He spoke no English and reeked heavily of onions.

He sat in the back seat with me, said nothing. After half an hour or so warming himself, he raised his hand to thank us, opened the door and disappeared into the whiteout of snow.

Nearly three decades later, I telephoned the two friends who had been in the car with me. Did this happen? Or did I dream it? Both vaguely remembered the man, although not the uniform, or the smell of onions. One recalled that the man abruptly disappeared into a snowdrift, as if he were a character in a deep dream.

The other wondered if we had conjured him: that part of the former Yugoslavia had also been heavily fought over in World War II; perhaps the old man was a ghost.

2. Confinement

I find myself, in these months of coronavirus confinement – mine taking place in France – in a similar mood to my wartime years, mainly in Yugoslavia. The French call it *le flottement* – floating.

For reasons I cannot explain, as I grow older, my memories of the past become more vibrant. And unlike my time in Sarajevo, here in the rural Alps I dream every night, with great precision and detail. Dead friends come back to me, speaking, give me specific messages.

'Why are you here?' I asked my much-loved and long-passed sister-in-law, Betsy, who in a dream sat on a chair next to me.

'Why would you ask a question like that at a time like this?' she responded, annoyed.

Another night my two dead brothers, Joseph and Richard, came together as children, building an enormous snow fort of ice. I could hear their childish laughter. My brother Joseph wore red mittens. I felt the cold of his soaked wet mitten pressing against my cheek. The past, my ancestors, seemed linked to me more than ever as my life ground to a halt and I watched the news of coronavirus spinning across the planet, destroying lives.

Seventeen years ago I married in this house, called Le Foyer, the ancient homestead of my ex-husband's family. It is in a part of France known as the Vercors, heavily fought over in World War II; in the garden is the grave of a relative shot by a German soldier in the final days before liberation.

The villages in this south-eastern part of France are small and remote; not unlovely but not chic. These homes are largely sturdy structures built for animals and their hard-working keepers. The

Alps hover; in the distance is Mont Aiguille, where the legend says mountaineering was developed in 1492, the year Christopher Columbus discovered America, displacing the Indigenous Native Americans.

On rainy days, the peak is hidden behind clouds; when the sun is out, I lie in the field and stare up at it, wondering who climbed it in the fifteenth century. It will be standing long after I am gone, my remains scattered in these fields, as I have asked my son to do, near a small chapel in the forest where I go daily to lay flowers at the feet of Our Lady.

How I once loved this place: the sound of a fountain outside my bedroom window where water from the mountain rushes; the quiet pace of a barn cat crossing a field sprouted with pink, yellow and pale blue wildflowers. When my husband and I separated, painfully, in 2008, my summer sojourns here came to an end.

I returned during the onset of the pandemic, taking an empty train from Gare de Lyon to Grenoble, and met my son, his father and three French cousins, who were children when I last saw them. Now they have grown to be competent adults: a mathematician; a political philosopher; a law student who wants to be a judge.

And while a dozen years have passed, when I opened a drawer in an upstairs bathroom, there was my old toothbrush and a jar of face cream, left behind. The rooms had not changed; inside a cupboard was scratched the name of a long-dead cousin: A. CAILLET. The heights of all the children going back to the 1930s were penciled onto a wall in the salon, including my own. I found the pink blanket with white polka dots which I had once put under a *tilleul* tree and used to hoist my laughing, infant son towards the cloudless perfect sky.

I settled into a relative's room, brushing cobwebs from the wooden bedposts, sleeping on musty linen sheets. Like millions of people, my life went into a holding pattern: a plane circling in a thick fog. In this case, it was months. It was not altogether unpleasant; I found comfort knowing others had done the same in their lives.

In 1942 Albert Camus travelled from Algeria to France, settling in the town of Chambon-sur-Lignon, on the other side of the Alps from where I am now. He suffered from chronic bouts of tuberculosis which left him weak, melancholic. He was separated from his wife; he missed the sun and smells of his native Algeria. He began to write *La Peste*, his allegory of occupied France, from his exile.

The infant I carried on walks through the fields is now a teenager, and left me to go on walks with his father exploring mountain passes; the cousins were at work on their various academic projects. Alone, I began to learn to see things in a way I never have before: flowers, earth, water. As weeks went by, and snowy March morphed into sunnier April and wet May, the farmers' tracts of land where they planted potatoes and turnips stretched from a small bit of brown earth to long patches of churned earth.

I studied objects intently. On the wall of the bedroom where I was staying is a drawing I have always loved. It's called *Le Retour au pays*. In it, a sailor sits in a country kitchen, not unlike the one here, with neighbors surrounding him.

He is regaling them with stories from a world far from their village. He sits on a stool surrounded by a priest, several women in clogs and headscarves, a young farmer with his hands on his knees, leaning toward him to hear of a world beyond the kitchen, the lit hearth, the bread on the table, the crucifix hung neatly on the wall.

3. *Déconfinement*

A few days before I decided to leave confinement, and take the train from Grenoble to Paris – I realized I needed to see more faces than the six people sheltering in Le Foyer and the local farmer, Benôit – my son called me to *la cave*.

The house has a series of underground rooms, which I imagine were used in the war, or as potato cellars. Now the space is divided into a wine cave, a children's playroom – the many cousins now grown with children of their own – and a room storing several dusty old church pews. Another room contains ancient farming equipment, jars of rope and plugs of every dimension, cans of nails and screws. My son had found an ancient VHS player, the kind we used in the 1990s and with it, he found six clunky tapes called JANINE'S WEDDING. The tapes looked old and clunky – who even has videos anymore? – and I suddenly remembered a documentary crew that had come to film the wedding for a future project on female war reporters, a film called *Bearing Witness*, which also featured my late friend and colleague Marie Colvin. t

I was pregnant and blooming – *épanouissement* as they say in French – and there were all my closest friends, seventeen years younger, recorded forever on a scratchy film. I had never watched these tapes – my pregnancy had been a difficult, though joyful one, and shortly after the wedding, I moved from London to Paris, and the tapes were displaced. Looking back on photos of the past has always been painful for me – my late father felt very much the same. The passage of time – his seven children's growth from infancy to adulthood, the losses and the sorrow that comes with life – was a terrible wound for him.

My son and I watched the videos, laughed at the speeches, observed the many who were no longer with us – my mountaineering father-in-law Philippe, who had died while skin diving in Tahiti in 2011, my dearest friend Roy who died of complications from Aids, an aunt called Tootsie, my mother's spirited older sister. There was my mother herself, now nearly 101 years old, wearing a sleeveless shift and Ray-Ban sunglasses, looking chic and youthful.

And there is my husband and myself, staring forward into a new life, underneath the gaze of Mont Aiguille. We did not know what was to come, and that knowledge saddened me.

I felt a tremendous sense of loss, but also, like that time in

Belgrade, a lifting, a release. The years I had believed were frozen and that would remain intact – the image of a younger woman holding her baby aloft on a pink blanket or in a white strapless wedding dress full of hope and joy – were somehow absorbed into the wrinkle of time.

I began to pack my things to end my confinement at Le Foyer, already suppressing the sense of nostalgia for a time that was lost. ∎

Quis est homo qui vi-
vet et non videbit
MORTEM.
PS. 88.

Haga-Comitis
ex Officina H. hondius
1642.

Horarum fallax MORS incertissima, rerum
Attamen Horarum cur tibi cura datur

THE FEARFUL SUMMER

Adam Nicolson

From April until July 1625: Huntingdon
Anno Regis Caroli 1°
Aetatis Suae XXV *to* XXVI

One afternoon late in April, by the pillory on Market Hill, as I stood with Alderman Stafford, considering whether we could set up some kind of workplace in which the able poor could earn their keep with flax or hemp, we watched the lunatic who lived out in Hartford come walking up the road from the bridge.

He wavered from one side of the street to the other, gutter to gutter, with his head twisted like a wryneck's on his body, & his hand up next to his chin, twisting & clutching at his ear as he walked.

Out of the way, a driver on a wagon muttered as he passed.

My only son has been eaten by a sow, the lunatic said when he reached us. All that was left of him after the sow had done her work was the stone in his heart.

He looked in the pocket of his breeches & held out a cobble on which the outline of a heart discoloured the stone.

My wife Johanne is so consumed with melancholy that she lies in a ditch & says she is dead.

He had been saying these things for two years but we had seen her every week at the cheese market as hale & pink as any woman in England. She cooked him & his son their bacon & eggs each morning & then sent her husband out on the road to tell us his repeated & mournful tale.

I took him back out to Hartford, talking along the way, cuckoos & woodpeckers in the woods, skylarks above us, cocks crowing in the yards. The whole world beside us was filled with people ploughing, hoeing, axing out the dead wood from the pollards, levelling molehills, cutting bean sticks, planting beans, raking old leaves, putting out dung. Women walked at the heads of the horses, the men behind with the ploughs. Pastures were being scoured with ox-drawn dredges, ploughlands broken up with horse-drawn harrows. The final cartloads of last summer's hay, which had been standing all winter in stacks out on the meadows, were being taken back to the barns before the cattle were let out on to the spring grazing. The only sound on the road was the oiled creak of the cart axles as they passed.

We came to the village. There was weeping in the roadway. The people there were wrapping a woman in a shroud. Beside her was the body of a boy in his. The woman had died that morning in a ditch. A man walking out to the fields had seen her as he passed. There had been a pig in the ditch too, gnawing at the body of the child who had died beside her. The lunatic stood next to the wrapped corpses of his wife & son & wailed like a demon in a play.

The next day a goose-drover was found dead, the geese, three or four hundred of them, milling around him, masterless, pecking at the hairs on his head & at the grass on the road up into Lincolnshire. A fisherman near Ramsey lay drowned in his nets with the carp & tench clustered at his face, their lips nibbling at his. The minister at Uplode fell from his pulpit, dropping on to the stones of the nave as he began with the words of his evening sermon, his text: 'Those who are first shall be last. Those who are up shall be down.' At the same moment all the myrtles & the jessamine in our garden withered & died. The oranges in their pots shrank & shrivelled. The almonds fell from the trees not only unripe but scarcely formed. An old ewe in Mepal gave birth to a three-headed ram lamb. It, they, lived & mewed, the three heads speaking one to the other for some hours, before all three died, one by one, a few minutes elapsing between the death of each, moments in which the living mourned long & pitifully their departed brothers. Later the lunatic from Hartford took ill, died & was buried next to his wife & child.

An insensate fear was in the town. A man, who had a boy in his house with all the signs of plague, turned him out & he went wandering & found himself taken in by an old & lonely widow & died that night in her house, where she then sickened too.

At the Council the tradesmen would not call it the plague for fear of losing custom. But they were overruled & we swore in a woman-searcher of the infected, to walk the streets to ask & hear where the sickness had come. The doors of those houses that were infected were to be nailed up. A red cross was to be set on the doors & the rubric LORD HAVE MERCY UPON US painted on the frame. We had a pesthouse made of boards & canvas out on the common between the mill & the bowling green & watchmen were set day & night to keep any from going there or coming thence. All that died in that house, or any house, were to be buried in the yard at St Benets.

Anyone in Huntingdon that had friends in the country that would receive them, into their houses, or a part of their houses, or even into a barn or a stable or a piggery, fled from the town as if from a fire, loading their goods & wares into carts & wagons, shouting at the men, bundling up the children, boarding up the doors & windows of their houses, as though a storm were coming. Thirty carts a day left Huntingdon piled high. House after house in the High Street & Bridge Street & Bear Lane & George Lane stood empty & lifeless as if blinded, blank to the world, with silence in the streets between them. The cats remained; the dogs had fled.

And so in truth I must confess, I sent away Beth & my mother & the children, down to Essex, to Stambridge & the Bourchiers, with all but four men from my household, not wanting to expose them to the violence of God's wrath. Dame Ann lent her coach to take them all.

As the children gathered at the foot of the coach steps, I kissed them on their heads & cheeks, & held their bodies, the ribs & shoulders, & brushed the curls of their hair. They were pleased to be going, with no fretfulness. Everything they knew was going with them.

Are we taking Bouncer? Richard asked.

No, not this time. He's staying with me.

And Trusty?

No, no, she's here too.

Soon, anyone of any standing had gone. Of the Council 24, I was very nearly the only one not to leave. There was none left who were ready to assist me & comfort the poor in their misery, neither recorder, justice, churchwarden nor overseers in all the town, nor high constable, but only two of the petty constables who had no friend to receive them in the country.

I had them come to stay with me & gave them ten shillings apiece by the week for their pains. Christopher Brathwaite & Jonas Pinhorn.

We spoke together late at night.

You have been sent from God to me, I told them.

Over a book of the Gospels we swore together that they would help me, both night & day, to help supervise & control the bearers who would carry the infected persons to the pesthouse in the town meadow & to help order the unruly people, who were ready both night & day to bring the place to ruin.

It was no festivity that meeting in the parlour by the light of our candle, with the shadows in the corners of the old room where the monks had prayed & conducted their ceremonies, before the light of Reformation. And we all made a vow & promised together that evening that whoever it pleased God to visit with his plague, the others would be faithful to him & would stay with him & tend to him in his suffering & dying.

In the light of the candle, I looked into their faces, as they did into mine, & all three of us knew we were looking into the grave.

A grave is no cavern of finality, I said to them. It is an arbour, an anteroom, as cool & shady as a summer parlour in a garden, where you will find peace & calm away from the trouble of this world. There you might rest from the heat of this life.

Not one of us believed those words, nor escaped their sorrow.

The people lived in pain before they died & for these paupers there was no escape. They burned & froze from one hour to the next, two days, three days before they succumbed. Their fingers darkened, their toes & feet & legs. Black noses on white faces.

They dragged the air in through their mouths as though breathing fog or water. I saw the bodies. They were blotched under the skin where the blood had clotted & pooled. I have never seen the dead so dead. All the goods in their houses were burned, all clothes & hangings, all the furniture & chests, every article in which the sickness might find its habitation.

Those who were not dead were dying. Those who were not dying were hungry. We had not enough to give them. And I knew before they came that they would soon make their complaints. At home I had the gateposts strengthened & the bar between them.

In the evening Richard Coulter the captain of the poor came to speak with me. I saw him coming & I stood at the gate to receive him, with Christopher & Jonas & the men of my house beside me.

He was a tall man with a spade of a beard & his body more sinew than flesh. His coat was wrapped around him with a rope at the waist & his cap low on his brow. He had worked much of his life at the peats, out in the fen &, once he was with me by the gate, he started to blaspheme.

Do you think we will be starved Oliver? Do you think your starving is what is right for the likes of us? Some kind of starving like that John Darlow, I believe you know him, found dead in the river last week, some way down from his house, starving but bloated as if he'd had his fill?

I said nothing.

You know we have no food? Coulter said.

We have done our best.

And sometimes the best is not enough. Not when you have the people starving like kittens in a puddle.

We can only get what the country provides.

What the country provides? & what of these houses here Oliver?

He pointed at the line of boarded-up buildings, the best houses in Huntingdon, going away towards the bridge.

Do you imagine the runaways have left behind anything in them houses which might, what could you say, be marketable?

And my house? I asked him.

Yours might be worth a rummage, Coulter said.

I thought of what little we had in there, what I had gathered in our lives, what my father had saved.

This man was the worst of any in Huntingdon, with the men & their women all round him, listening to him, jeering with him, mocking.

You lost last time we played at the tables, did you not? & I am not certain you are on a winning streak now.

I walked up close to him, saying nothing but looking at him until I was near enough to hit him but I feinted & then, as I always intended, as he ducked I grabbed him by the collar & held him down like a boy, head down, as he wrestled to get out of the hold but my men were on to him, holding him down, pushing him further into the dung of the road, so that he was held by their weight to his knees & then on to his chest & belly, where I could ask him where he might like to play the next round?

His others around him were shouting & roaring.

Not here I think, I said. Nor in the Falcon, where the ale has never been to my liking. But I have an idea where the drink might be to your taste.

With Christopher & Jonas binding him with his own rope I took him to the gaol & threw him in there with the others on the straw in the strong room at the back & promised them a whipping.

Death was coming into the houses without complaint or fanfare & most of the people began to die in a sort of quiet.

One man, though, we could hear him shouting in Corbet's Lane at the top of the town, a crowd of others gathered outside his bolted door. He was speaking of his money, saying that this person & that owed him a thousand pounds, until his brother came & talked to him through the barred-up door & prayed that he would lay aside all earthly cares & trust that he was about to go to the place where his forefathers had gone.

Earth, earth, dust, dust, the dying man came to say. All things are toys & trifles. When can we leave this turmoil & corruption?

As they died I had the bearers carry the dead to the graveyard & the living of their families to the pesthouse on the common.

Bearers were not easy to find. I could get only three to carry at first. Each of them asked four shillings for the service & only with that in their pockets did they take their loads. In the churchyard were two tenements. I put the three bearers in one of them, just the men. Their families stayed in their own places.

In the dark that night, with the braziers burning where the men were keeping watch over the houses still occupied & those that were empty, the lights of their fires shone & wavered up & down the streets.

I was at home when a woman came running & told me that her neighbour Robert Belman had come to her house & pulled her out of it with all her goods into the road & told her to leave the house & leave the town because she was wife to one of the bearers.

I gathered my coat & men & staff & sword & went to find this Belman. He was sitting in the half-dark with a tallow light at the back of his rooms.

Why did you push that poor woman out of doors & all her goods?

I won't have her there, he said.

And why is that?

I know her husband will come to her in the night, & what will he bring with him? Sickness from the bodies he has been handling all day. And the two of them, this woman & that man her husband, they are not of the best. They never have been & we have always heard them next door late at night, contesting & blaspheming & taking the

Lord's name in vain. And worse I can tell you. It will be no surprise to me or Mrs Belman if God's will condemns them to this death. And if them, then in all likelihood us. The sickness has no respect for walls.

You must allow her back. And take down the barricade you have made at her door & help her in with her goods.

I will not. She is not to return.

I collared him & had him bound by Christopher & Jonas & we began to walk & half drag him to the gaol.

We were halfway down the High Street, almost at the gaol. But then the people were gathering & we were surrounded in the dark by a crowd of them, of his friends, telling me, their mouths up next to me, that I had no right to imprison him, pushing & joshing at me, gales of their breath all over me in the dark like a pack of hounds at the lights & skirts of a piece of meat, slavering in their anger, walking backwards in front of me, fingers in my face, shouting all over me in a fog of noise, but I would have none of it. Leave me or I will imprison you all, I said & collared first one & then another, having them bound so that their arms were held close to their sides.

At last, after that, we got the woman into her house.

I saw her settled & her goods set out in the rooms, her bed restrung & the bedclothes on it, her kissing my hand & full of gratitude to me. But no rest in this time of trouble. I was back at home when the three bearers came running.

Mr Fragg had brought a crowd of citizens to their house in the graveyard. They had been beating on the walls of the house. They were raging & bellowing beyond the doors & walls, singing & shouting, hate & fear: If you don't come out we'll pull it down around you.

A gang of them had collected at one of the corner posts of the house & begun to rock it back & forth so that the whole house started to shudder & shift. Tiles fell from the roof into the street & split there. The gutter broke from its fixings. Glass in the casements upstairs splintered from the frames & fell in pieces on the road below. And so the bearers, with fear in their hearts, cried out to the mob to stop, shouting through the closed door & asked that they might be given free & quiet passage away from the churchyard & to me. And so here they were now & what was I to do?

It was the Sabbath after candlelight.

We shall be killed, the bearer said. Take us away. Only you can save us. Matthew Fragg brought more than three hundred of them to our door, all of them with death in their hearts. They have been taking the fallen tiles & throwing them through the windows of our house. They have lit a fire outside & threatened us with death by burning. They have boiled cauldrons & pans of water on their fire & thrown the scalding water in on us. Look.

He showed his hand & arm.

With my staff, & a sword at my side, I went down in the dark late in the night, along with my men, to the house. No one saw us on the way & we put the three of them back in.

No sooner were they there than the mob gathered again. The whole town of Huntingdon was there, breathing like a beast, heavy in the dark, as if it were a body in trouble, the hectic in its veins. Look down one alley & there were men running one way, shadows in the lit patches, down another & a crowd gathering like a clot or an imposthume in the blood, the whole body of the town diseased & discomposed, death in its limbs, burning with fever, red & swollen with hatred & fear.

Mr Fragg was with the crowd of others in the flare light, the light coming & going on their faces. I knew him from the Council well enough. We had laughed & joked a little about sir Oliver & dame Ann, his belly, her cakes. He had been, I thought, my friend.

They are not to stay here, Fragg said, & pushed at me with his fists against my chest, thinking to bowl me over.

If you do that again I will have you in the gutter, I said & pushed back at him, hard with the heels of my hands, so that he staggered into the mass of bodies behind him, arms out, caught by them before he fell.

His friend & ally there, a man who had worked for him, a tanner, Lancelot Russell, saw us in this argument & drew his sword, & if God in his mercy had not prevented his thrust by the hand of Jonas the constable, he would have run me through & I would have died there that night in the fear that was on us.

Holding on to Christopher Brathwaite's neck beside me, urgently, speaking in his ear, I said to him, We have to still this, we have to bring some peace to this, some obedience, some order here now or more men will die than need. Make a proclamation now, yes four times, to still the noise.

O yeas! O yeas! O yeas! O yeas! Brathwaite began, deep & clanging above them, a pealing bell from his height above us. Hear me now!

I looked at him beside me, crowing as a cockerel high above the run where the hens crowded & clustered in their worry.

The Bailiff doth straitly charge all men & all manner of people in the King's Majesty's name, that hath not to do here, by the command of him & the Common Council of this borough presently to depart upon pain of imprisonment.

Nothing happened. The dark crowd of men rustled like leaves in a wind. I went close up to Mr Fragg.

Will you be gone? I require you to return to your house.

Me?

Yes, you. You have managed & gathered a violent & wicked rout of men to batten on the people & those who in our time of trouble are doing all that we can to keep the good order of this borough. So go. If I need to say it one more time & you are not gone, I will lay you here in the street as good as I am God's servant.

He did not go. I asked Brathwaite to call again, to calm that stirring sea.

O yeas! O yeas! Brathwaite sang again, his church voice echoing above us. Hear me now!

Mr Fragg stood there with Russell beside him, fixed & planted on the graveyard earth.

I hit Fragg as he smiled at me, my fist in his teeth, the bones of my fingers on the bones of his face, what felt like bone on stone, no give in him, no flesh, & he fell as a log at my feet, his eyes shut, his mouth open, the blood in his mouth a bright pool between his lips.

Get up! I said.

But he lay there & the others thought I had killed him in rage & so they went & vanished up the streets of the town & away behind their doors into their houses & the dark.

Jonas threw a pail of water on Fragg's face, twice, & another over his body to wake him. Russell stood by, hand on hilt. Fragg groaned, felt his mouth, looked up at me, sat, considered where he was, pushed himself to his feet, no looking at me now, & held by Russell went off to his house, no words between us.

Then at least the town was quiet, the bearers were in where I needed them to be. My fingers were swelling.

One woman, Goody Good, shouted from her window above us as we passed home up Mill Lane: You are not worth a hedgehog's turd Mr Bailiff. You & the slodger girls. I know of your antics.

We broke her door, I had her bound & Jonas & Christopher threw her to the cage with the others.

The night passed & in the morning a quiet lay on the empty streets. The people away in the country. A glowing dawn. The houses boarded up. One cock crew. A cat picked at the rubbish by the bridge house on the quay. That morning the alms of bread & beer were given to the poor. The carts were coming as I had ordered with the quarters of wheat & barley already ground, the bakers at work, the brewers bringing in the hogsheads of half-crown ale.

And so for a few days it was quiet. Until the bearers of the dead went in rebellion.

They came to my gate. One of my men, Jack Raveley said there were three of them waiting. I said for them to come up but he told me they would not. I went down & found them at the gate, each of them with a good hedge stake in his hand.

What is it with you here?

We need money; we will not do this for four shillings.

I stepped down by them & said: You shall have something.

I called for my men & boys. Together we picked stones from the street. When we were ready, we began to stone the bearers, a hailstorm on their heads.

The bearers, retreating ten yards, gathered stones themselves & tried as best they could to throw them at us but it was God's will that a stone of mine landed clear in the middle of one of their heads, felling him there, until he stumbled up & away, hand to his head, & the others ran after him. We followed them until they were driven back into their house in the churchyard where they cowered unseen behind the wooden walls.

Raveley had brought his musket. I had him charge it with a pair of bullets. I told the bearers, You dally with me but I am in earnest. Do what you have said you will do for four shillings. Not one of you before has had more than a shilling a month.

From beyond the walls one answered: We will not.

Then you should pray, as you will die.

I had my man shoot his musket through their window. Once. And then again. And then again. And then again. And then at the door. And then at the tiles on the edge of the roof. And then the window again. And again. And again. And again. All glass was broken, the wood splintered. And at the tenth time, the bearers' spokesman cried out to me to let them live. They would do what they should do, if I could give them a Bible & a clean shirt each. I promised them that & left them. The people that had gathered outside the churchyard at the sound of the musket withdrew before us like sheep before dogs.

The sickness lived on with us. One man, John Digges, in his despair or confusion mixed white arsenic with a dish of food for his wife & all his household. All ate & all died, he the last among them after he had seen them sup their fill.

Another, Richard Dawson, knowing he was sick & seeing that he must die of it, stood up out of his bed & dug his own grave, asking his nephew John Dawson to throw some straw in there, & when it was done he went & laid down in that grave, & asked for his bedclothes to be laid on him & there he died & departed out of this world. To his nephew he said he did it because he was a large & strong man & heavier than John & his brother could bury.

Another, Jonathan Bull, a wood-cleaver, lived in a small tenement, just one storey, in Cobbler's Lane, with a little door to the street & a window beside it.

A passer-by said she heard the wife crying out in distress & so I went to the door of his house & asked her through it:

How is it with you & your husband, & your children?

They cannot speak to me, she said. The sickness has stolen their voices. They are lying here beside me now. And she sank in silence.

I told her that in the night they would all be removed to the pesthouse, & she must provide everything she wanted carried with them.

No you cannot, she said to me, whispering at the door. You cannot do that to me or to us. I will not have them die in the pesthouse. If they are going to die they will die here. You have no right. If you take us we shall all die.

Late in the night I came to have them out, but she would not open the door & again she railed at me.

Are you born of a woman or a beast that you should do so bloody an act upon people in our suffering condition? Are you the Devil's spawn?

I told the bearers to break the house open but they would not or could not. So I sent my man home for my iron bar. Still she would not open & so I gave the bearers orders to drive the bar in between the door posts & the door itself & at the second stroke they burst it. Two of the bearers went in but no sooner in than they were out in the lane again.

Do you not know that our lives are as precious to us as yours is to you? the bearer asked. We will not go in. The house is hot. Feel it. You can feel the heat coming out through the door like the contagion itself. That smell is the smell of death. And the house is burning up with the heat of the infection.

You have no choice, I said.

And again, standing back a few yards away across the lane, together with my men we beat them with stones so that they were forced into the house for shelter. And so they brought out these three speechless people & the woman still railing at us as the Devil's own serpents, the worms of hell, & carried them into the fields to the pesthouse, her crying every step of the way, & even on after we had locked them in with the others.

What can be done save that which must be done? What is necessity in a cruel world? Is necessity not just another name for God? Or is he God's brother who does his cruellest work? As water falls from a leat into a millpond & from the pond on to the wheel & from the wheel out into the after-race, God's will is in the world. What are we but bubbles on the stream of his being?

The evenings passed & the fire-filled nights. The possessions of all those who died were burned in the streets. We killed the dogs & trapped the rats & cats. Only Bouncer & Trustlove stayed with me, kept within the gates at home. And Huntingdon was a town of death. One in three of those in the pesthouse died & was buried. It was not long before these bearers of the dead began to lose their minds. One evening I came to the place beside the burying ground out beyond the castle ruins where I could see & hear them, each of them carrying on their shoulders a two-quart pot of ale. The searching-woman was with them, carrying her own pot above her like that, as if she were the verger & they her priests. The four of them were dancing among the graves & singing,

> Shoulder-work, oh shoulder-work
> Is there any better than shoulder-work?

carrying the pots of ale to the newly covered graves & with ceremony & singing placing them on the earth, before drinking from them to the point where they staggered & fell & lay down by the dead.

I did not come too close, on that midnight, but I could hear the music of their pipes & tambourines, & see them dancing by the bonfire, man & woman, it could have been a kind of matrimony, or a stately sacrament. Two & two they danced, holding each other by hand or arm. Round the fire they joined in circles, their laughter burning up & out above the flames, beside the falling logs of the fires, bitter mirth in their faces, their bodies & feet following the slow music in the shadows, feet rising & falling, all in the rhythm of dancing & drinking, grief & death. ■

CLEMENTINE, CARMELITA, DOG

David Means

A middle-aged dachshund with a short-haired, caramel-colored coat, scurried along a path, nervously veering from one side to the other, stopping to lower her nose to the ground, to catch traces of human footwear, a whiff of rubber, an even fainter residue of shoe leather, smells that formed a vague pattern of hikers in the past. Some had probably walked through that part of the woods long ago. She lifted her nose and let it flare to catch the wind from the north, and in it she detected the familiar scent of river water after it had passed through trees and over rock, a delightful and – under other circumstances – soothing smell that in the past had arrived to her in the house when her person, Norman, opened the windows.

The wind was stirring the trees, mottling the sunlight, and she tweezed it apart to find his scent, or even her own scent, which she'd lost track of in her burst of freedom. But all she caught was a raccoon she knew and a whiff of bacon frying in some faraway kitchen, so she put her nose down and continued north again, following an even narrower path – invisible to the human eye – into thick weeds and brush, picking up burrs as she moved into the shadows of the cliffs to her left until the ground became hard and rocky.

Then she paused for a moment and lifted her head and twitched her ears to listen for a whistle, or the sound of her own name, Clementine, in Norman's distinctive pitch. All she heard was the rustle of leaves, the call of birds. How had she gotten into this predicament, her belly low to the ground, lost in a forest?

That morning Norman had jiggled the leash over her head, a delightful sound, and asked her if she wanted to go for a walk – as if she needed to be asked – and looked down as she danced and wagged and rushed to the back door to scratch and bark. At the door, she had sniffed at the crack where the outside air slipped in and, as she had many times before, caught the smell that would never leave the house, the mix of patchouli and ginger that was Claire. She was still Claire's dog. In the scent was a memory of being lifted into arms and nuzzled and kissed – the waxy lipstick – and then other memories of being on the floor, rolling around, and then the stark, earthy smell that she'd noticed one day near Claire's armpit, a scent she knew from an old friend, a lumbering gray-furred beast who was often tied up outside the coffee shop in town. It was the smell of death. Claire got that smell seeping up through her skin. It became stronger and appeared in other places until she began sleeping downstairs in the living room, in a bed that moaned loudly when it moved, and there were days on that bed, sleeping in the sun at her feet, or in her arms, and then, in the strange way of humans, she disappeared completely.

When Claire was gone, Norman began to give off his own sad odor of metal and salt, and Clementine did everything she could to make him happy, grabbing his balled socks out of the laundry pile and tossing them in the air, rolling to expose her belly when he approached, leaning against him as he read on the couch, until she began to carry her own grief.

This morning he'd dangled the leash and while she was waiting at the back door, he'd gone to the kitchen and got a tool from a drawer, an oil and saltpeter thing that made a frightening sound, Clementine knew, because once he had taken her along to shoot it upstate. (Don't get me wrong. She knew it was a gun but she didn't have a name for it – it was an object that had frightened her.) The thing was zipped into his bag when he came to the door. He stood with his hand on the handle, and she waited while he looked at the kitchen for a few seconds – minutes, in dog time – and then she was pulling at the leash, feeling the fresh air and the sun and the morning dew as she guided him along the road, deep in routine, barely bothering with the roadside odors, to the entrance of the park. On the main path that morning – with the water to the right and the woods to the left – there had been the usual familiar dogs, some passing with their noses to the ground, snobbishly, others barking a greeting. (Her own mode was to bark as if they were a threat – she was, after all, as she acknowledged in these moments, shorter than most dogs – while also wagging vigorously at the same time.) There had been an old Irish setter, Franklin, who had passed her with a nod, and then a fellow dachshund named Bonnie, who had also passed without much of a greeting, and then finally Piper, an elderly retired greyhound who had stopped to say hello while his person and Norman spoke in subdued voices – she got the tone of sadness, picked up on it – and then, when the talk was over, Norman had pulled her away from Piper and they continued up the path until they came upon a small, nameless mixed-breed mutt who launched, unprovoked, into a crazy tail-chasing routine in the middle of the path, a dervish stirring up the dust in a way that made Clementine step away and pull on the leash, because it is a fact that there is just as much nonsense in the dog world as there is in the human world.

Sitting now on the rocky ground resting, she lifted her nose to the wind and caught the smell of a bear in a cloak of limestone dust from the quarry, and inside the same cloak was the raccoon she knew, the one that had rummaged around Norman's garbage cans, and then, of course, deer – they were everywhere. Lacking anything better to do, she put her nose down and began to follow deer traces along the rocks and into the grass, a single-file line of hooves that led to a grove of pines where they had scattered, broken in all directions, and at this spot she cried softly and hunched down, feeling for the first time what might (in human terms) be called fear, but was manifested instinctually as a riffle along her spine that ran through the same fibers that raised her hackles, and then, for a second, smelling pine sap, she closed her eyes and saw the basement workshop where she sometimes stood and watched Norman, until one of his machines made a sound that hurt her ears and sent her scurrying up the stairs.

Cold was falling and her ears twitched at the memory of the sound of the saw blade. Norman was upstairs in his room staring ahead and clicking plastic keys in front of a glowing screen while she lay on old towels in the sunlight, waiting for the clicking to stop, opening her eyes when it did and searching for a sign that he might get up, get her food. Sometimes his voice rose and fell while she sat at his feet and looked up attentively, raising her paws when he stopped. Since Claire had disappeared, he left the house in the morning only to return at night, in the dark, to pour dry kibble – that senseless food – into her dish and splash water into her drinking bowl. Behind his door, the television droned and maybe, on the way out of the house the next morning, he might reach down and ruffle her head and say, 'I'm sorry, girl, I'm not such great company these days.'

As she opened her eyes, stood up, and began walking, these memories were like wind against her fur, telling her where she should be instead of where she was at that moment, moving north through the trees. The sun had disappeared behind the cliffs and dark shadows spread across the river and the wind began to gust, bringing geese and scrub grass, tundra and stone – wrapped in a shroud from beyond the Arctic Circle, an icy underscent that foretold the brutality of missing vegetation; it was a smell that got animals foraging and eating, and it made her belly tense.

Here I should stress that dog memory is not at all like human memory, and that human memory, from a dog's point of view, would seem strange, clunky, unnatural and deceptive. Dog memory isn't constructed along temporal lines, gridded out along a distorted timeline, but rather in an overlapping and, of course, deeply olfactory manner, like a fanned-out deck of cards, perhaps, except that the overlapping areas aren't hidden but are instead more intense, so that the quick flash of a squirrel in the corner of the yard, or the crisp sound of a bag of kibble being shaken, can overlap with the single recognizable bark of a schnauzer from a few blocks away on a moonlit night. In this account, as much as possible, dog has been translated into human, and like any such translation, the human version is a thin, feeble approximation of what transpired in Clementine's mind as she stood in the woods crying and hungry, old sensations overlapping with new ones, the different sounds that Norman's steps had made that morning, the odd sway of his gait, and the beautiful smell of a clump of onion grass – her favorite thing in the world! – as she'd deliriously sniffed and sneezed, storing the smell in the chambers of her nose for later examination while Norman waited with unusual patience.

That smell of onion grass was the last thing she could remember – again in that overlapping way – along with a small herd of deer, who that morning had been a few yards away in the woods, giving off a funk, and the sudden freedom around her neck when Norman unharnessed her and took the leash and she darted up into the woods, running past the place where the deer had been and, on the way, catching sight of the rabbit for the first time, chasing it while feeling herself inside a familiar dynamic that worked like this: he would let her go and she'd feel the freedom around her neck, running, and then at some point he would call her name, or, if that didn't work, whistle to bring her back; each time she'd bound and leap and tear up the hillside and then, when he called, she'd find herself between two states: the desire to keep going and the desire to return to Norman, and each time she'd keep running until he called her name again, or whistled. Then she'd retrace her own scent to find her way back to him.

It was true that since Claire had disappeared the sound of his whistle had grown slack, lower in tone, but he always whistled, and when she returned there was always a flash of joy at the reunion. Not long ago, he'd swept her into his arms and smothered her with his blessing, saying, *good girl, good girl, what did you find up there?*

Then with great ceremony he'd rolled her up into his arms, kissed her, plucked a burr from her coat, and carried her over the stones to the waterline where he let her taste and smell an underworld she would never know: eels, seagrass, fish and even the moon.

Yes, in the morning light she'd caught sight of a cottontail flash of white in the trees and then, giving chase, barking as she ran, followed it into the brush until she came to it in a clearing, brown with a white tail, ears straight up, frozen in place, offering a pure but confusing temptation. There they stood, the two of them. His big eyes stared into her big eyes. The rabbit darted sharply and Clementine was running with the grass thrashing her belly and then, faster, with all four paws leaving the ground with each stretched-out bound. There was nothing like those bounds! Slowed down in dog time it was a sublime joy, the haunches tightening, spreading out and then coiling – she could feel this sensation! – as the rabbit zigzagged at sharp angles and, at some point, dashed over a creek while she followed, leaping over the water to the other side where, just as fast as it had appeared, the rabbit vanished, finding a cove, or a warren hole in the rocks at the bottom of the palisade, leaving her with a wagging tail and a wet nose and lost for the first time in her life.

Now she was alone in the dark, making a bed in the pine needles, circling a few times and then lowering her nose on her paws, doing her best to stay awake while the cool air fell onto her back. Out of habit, she got up and circled again in place and then lay down, keeping her eyes open, twitching her eyebrows, closing them and then opening them until she was in the room with Norman, who was at his desk working, clicking his keys. Claire was there, reaching down and digging her thumb into a sweet spot where the fur gave around her neck.

Hearing a sound, she opened her eyes. There were patches of underworld moonlight and through them deer were moving quietly. The bear was still to the north in the wind. A skunk was spreading like ink.

In the car with Norman and Claire, her own face was at the open window, the wind lifting her ears, and her nose was thrust into a fantastic blast of beach and salt marsh and milkweed chaff while, in the front seat, they talked musically to each other, singing the way they used to sing.

Something rustled in the woods. In the faint starlight, the large shadow of the bear moved through the trees. She kept still and watched until it was devoured by the dark.

She was in the bed by the window in Norman's room. He was tapping the keys. Tap tap, tap, tap.

The tapping arrived in morning light. It came from a stick against the forest floor.

The man holding the stick was tall and lean with a small blue cap on his head. *Hey, good dog, good doggie, what are you doing out here, are you lost?* The flat of his palm offered something like coconut, wheat flour, hemp and, as an underscent, the appealing smell of spicy meat.

The man picked her up gently and carried her – *How long have you been up here, what's your name, girl?* – across the ridge of stones, through the woods to a wider path under big trees and then down, over several large stones, to the beach where he smoked and poured some water into a cup and laughed as she lapped it up, twirling her tongue into her mouth. In his hand was a piece of meat, spicy and sweet as she gulped it down, and then another, tossed lightly so that she could take it out of the air, not chewing it at all, swallowing it whole.

That was all it took. One bit of spicy meat and she reconfigured her relationship with the human. She felt this in her body, in her haunches, her tail, and the taste of the meat in the back of her throat. But, again, it wasn't so simple. Again, this is only a translation, as close as one can get in human terms to her thinking at this moment, after the feeling of the cold water on her tongue and the taste of meat. One or two bits of meat aren't enough to establish a relationship. Yes, the moment the meat hit her mouth a new dynamic was established between this unknown person and herself, but, to put it in human terms, there was simply the *potential* in the taste of meat for future tastes of meat. The human concept of *trust* had in no way entered the dynamic yet, and she remained ready to snap at this strange man's hand, to growl, or even, if necessary, to growl and snap and raise her hackles and make a run for it. Human trust was careless and quick, often based on silly – in canine terms – externals, full of the folly of human emotion.

This is as good a place as any to note that through all of her adventures, from the early-morning walk on the path to the long trek through the woods and the night in the pine needles, Clementine did not once hear the loud report of a gun. Of course she wasn't anticipating the sound. Once the gun was in Norman's bag, it was gone from her mind, completely, naturally. It wasn't some kind of Chekhovian device that would have to, at some point, go off.

The man picked her up from the sand, brushed her paws clean – *It's gonna be okay. Where do you live?* – and carried her to the main trail. The sway of his arms made her eyes close. When she opened them, they were on a road and the limestone dust was strong, and there was a near-at-hand bacon smell coming from a house. He put her down and let her clamber down a small, cinder-block stairway and through a door and into his house.

In a charged emotional state, Clementine poked around the strange rooms sniffing the corners, eagerly reconnoitering – a dusty stuffed seal under a crib in a room upstairs, eatable crumbs under a bed, a cinnamon candle near a side table, a long row of records – all the while missing the freedom she had experienced in the woods, bounding through the trees, the harness gone, and beneath that, a feeling that Norman somewhere outside was still calling her name, or whistling.

All day she explored the house, pausing for naps in the afternoon sun, and retraced the activities of previous dogs, a long-ago cat and various persons. She found pill bugs and cobwebs (she hated cobwebs) in the corners, and on a chair in the dining room, small plastic bags of something similar to skunk grass and spider flowers – not exactly onion grass, but still worth close attention.

That day, Clementine came to understand that the man's name was Steve. Later in the afternoon, a woman named Luisa arrived and spoke a different language – no words like *sit*, or *walk*, or *good dog*, or *hungry* – to which she paid close attention, partly because Luisa had a smell similar to Claire's, gingery and floral with a faint verdant bready odor that – Clementine felt this, in her dog way – united them in a special way. There was also the way Luisa rubbed her neck, gently and then more firmly, using her thumb as she leaned down and said, *What should we call you?* And then went through many beautiful words until she settled on *Carmelita*. *Carmelita,* she said. *Carmelita.*

Even in her excitement over her new home, Carmelita was experiencing a form of grief particular to her species. There are fifty-seven varieties of dog grief, just as there are – from a dog's point of view – 110 distinct varieties of human grief, ranging from a vague gloom of Sunday-afternoon sadness, for example, to the intense, peppery, lost-father grief, to the grief she was smelling in this new house, which was a lost child (or lost pup) type of grief, patches of which could be found in the kitchen, around the cabinets, near the sink, and all over the person named Luisa. It was on the toys upstairs, too, and as she sniffed around she gathered pieces together and incorporated them into her own mood.

Resting in the moonlight that night, on an old blanket in the room with the stereo speakers, she kept her eyes open. An owl hooted outside. A faraway dog barked. A distant rumble sound, along with a high screeching sound, began in the distance and gradually grew into a high-pitched screeching and clattering, a booming roar that was worse than thunder, and then it tapered off, pulled itself away into the distance, and disappeared.

The light came on and Steve rubbed her belly – *It's just a train, sweetie, you'll have to get used to those* – and then, in the dark again, she detected a mouse in the corner, erect on two feet, holding and nibbling on something. When she growled it disappeared into the wall. The light came again and Luisa rubbed her head and belly. Then it was dark again and to soothe herself she brought out from one of the chambers in her nose the smell of onion grass.

D ays passed. Weeks passed. Carmelita settled into her new life. Some days, Luisa was in the house, moving around, sitting at the table with the smell of green stuff, dangling a bag of it in front of Carmelita's nose so she could sniff and open her mouth and gently clasp – she had learned not to bite the bags.

One afternoon, Steve took her into the woods, along a small trail, and through a fence to an open spot. She lay and watched as he dug with a shovel, cut down stalks, and stopped to smoke. (She liked to snap at the rings he made, to thrust her nose into the smell that tangled up and brought the sudden overlap of memory: Claire in her bed smoking, and the strange smell of the cans under the workbench in Norman's workshop.)

In the evenings, they ate at the table in candlelight and talked about someone named Carmen. Each time the word appeared, the smell of grief would fill the room. The scent was all over the house, in different variations. She even found it on the thing that Steve carried when he left the house in the morning, a leather satchel with a bouquet of iron and steel, clinking when he hefted it up – *So long, Carmelita,̓ see you after work, gotta go build something* – an object always worth examining when he came back to the house because it carried an interesting array of distant places, and other humans.

Sometimes they took her for a walk to the woods, or down the road past the stone quarry to a park where children played and other dogs hung out. She became friendly with the dogs there and they exchanged scents and greetings. Her favorite, Alvy, a bulldog with a playful disposition and a scratching issue, came to the house one evening and they slept together in her bed, side by side. He snorted and sneezed and coughed in his sleep. When he sneezed – his massive nose was beautiful – he emitted a cornucopia of aromas, mint weed, leathery jerky Arctic vegetation, even a hint of caribou – essences he had drawn in from the northern wind and stored for future examination.

Winter came. Snow fell. The ice smell from the north became the smell outside. When Carmelita went out in the evening – her belly brushing the snow – she kept to the path and did her business quickly, stopping only for a moment to taste the air. Then she dashed back to Steve in the doorway, the warmth of the house pouring around him into the cold blue.

One night there were cries from the bedroom upstairs. She got up – noting the mouse – and went and saw them naked together, wrapped in the familiar bloom of salt and, somehow, a fragrance like the river underworld. When they were finished they brought her up onto the bed. There was a hint of spring in the air that night, and the next morning; the wind shifted and the ice smell from the north was replaced by southern smells – one day faint forsythia and crocus, another day Spanish moss and dogwood, magnolia, morning glories, and another the addition of redbuds, and, of course, cypress, all these smells drifting in a *mirepoix* (no other human word will do) of red clay and turned rich farm soil that told the animal world that green was coming. When the weather was good she would go out to the back deck – passing through the little door Steve had installed – and rest her chin on the wooden rail, looking out over the water, watching the birds in the sky, as she turned the wind around in her nose.

One morning there was another presence in the house, a small thump in Luisa's belly, a movement. Carmelita put her head down and listened, hearing a white liquid fury, along with the thump, while her tongue – licking and licking Luisa's skin – tasted the tangy salt of new life.

That night she woke in darkness – the moon gone, no moon at all – to the sound of a raccoon crying. Through the window over her bed the strong southern wind slipstreamed, and when she fell back asleep she was free, chasing the rabbit (if you had been in the room, you'd have seen her paws twitching as she lay on her side), bounding through soft grass, inside the pursuit. The rabbit froze, ears straight and still, and offered its big, pooling eyes. They stood in the clearing for a moment, Carmelita on one side, the rabbit on the other. The air was clear and bright and the sun was warm overhead. Then the rabbit spoke in the language of dog. The rabbit spoke of the sadness Carmelita sometimes felt, a long stretched-out sense of displacement that would arrive, suddenly, amid the hubbub of the house, the leather satchel fragrance, the thump in Luisa's skin – that heartbeat – and the memory of Claire. It spoke loudly of all the things that had gone into the past and all of the things that might, like a slice of meat, appear in the future, and then it dashed off to one side, heading toward a mountain, and with a bark (Carmelita did bark, giving a dreamy snap of her jaw) she was back in the chase, moving in gravity-free bounds over velvety grass until, with a start, she woke to darkness, staring around the room – a faint residual pre-dawn marking the windows and, once again, the mouse on its hind legs, holding something as it gently nibbled.

The end of spring came and the air filled with a superabundance of local trees, grasses, flowers and pollen. Some days, the air was neither north nor south. A newborn was in the house, too, gurgling and twisting, crying at night.

One afternoon, the house quiet, Carmelita went onto the deck to air and sun. At the railing, her chin on the wood, she examined the wind coming from the south and as she sniffed she caught and held Norman's smell. It was faint. In human terms it was not a smell at all – a microscopic tumbleweed of his molecules. But it was there. She caught it and held it in her nose, in one of the chambers, and turned it over like a gemstone.

That night the rabbit did not pause at the end of the glade and instead the chase went on and on, weaving around until she woke up in the darkness and to soothe herself, she sat up and examined the little bit of Norman's smell she had stored in her nose. (Again, this is just a translation. There wasn't, in any of this, a concept of causality, and the smell of Norman in the air alone, mixed into a billion other smells, wasn't enough to make her dream of escaping to the woods to trace her way back to her previous origin point. She was perfectly content in her life with Steve and Luisa and the baby, walks in the woods, good food, lots of fresh meat, even on occasion the spicy meat. That tiny bundle of molecules that smelled like Norman was just something to ponder, to bring back out.) Dawn was breaking and she got up and went to the bedroom, clicking her long nails, to listen to Steve and the baby.

One night in August she was chasing the rabbit again, a ball of white movement that pulled her along a stretch of the main path that she had travelled many times. As she ran she passed familiar pee-spots: picnic-bench legs, trash cans, bushes. The rabbit didn't zig, or zag, but was running in a straight line, undaunted, and because of this she felt a new kind of fury, an eagerness that drove her across the wide parking lot, past cars and people, with the wide river glassy and quivering to the left of her vision – everything in a dreamlike way pulled into the vortex of her singular desire, nothing at all playful this time, so that she kept her head down and plunged ahead. Then she was up the hill – completely familiar – and along a stone path to the door of the house where the rabbit had stopped and turned, twitching, standing still, as if offering itself to her. In a single fluid motion she clutched it in her rear paw, twisting hard and then, when she had her chance, she got to the rabbit's neck, clamped down, and shook it until it stopped moving and then shook it some more, taking great pleasure in its resistance to the motion of *her* neck, and then, as she was tasting the bloody meat, gamey and warm, there was the sound of Steve speaking, and she was on her blanket, which she had pawed all the way across the room. It was morning. He was in the doorway to the kitchen with a mug of coffee in his hand. *You must've been dreaming,* he said. *Your little paws were moving.*

Did one dream foretell another? Was it possible that the dream indicated what was to come? Of course she would never think of it that way because she wasn't bound by the logic of causality; the dream of the rabbit was as real as her waking state, so it overlapped with what happened one afternoon, a Saturday late in the summer, when Steve took her for a long hike along the path. (He never took her too far down the path because he didn't want to give her up. He had made a half-hearted attempt to locate her owner, asking around, looking at posts on the internet, until he was persuaded that no one in the area had reported a missing dachshund. But then one day at the Stop & Shop on Mountain Road, on the community bulletin board, he saw her photo. But by the summer, the dog was part of the family, and it seemed important – in some mystical way – that she had appeared in the woods before Luisa became pregnant.)

Once again it seems important to stress that Carmelita's world is composed of fibers of sensation caught like lint in a web of her neurons, a vivid collection of tastes, luminous visions, dreams, and even, in her own ways, hopes and grief. Enter her nose, the enfolded sensors a million times more sensitive to odor than your own; imagine what it was like for her to hold, even as a clump of molecules, the distinctive smell of Norman, along with every thing she had ever encountered arrayed like a nebula swirl, spinning in a timeless location.

On the path, she pulled on the leash, feeling big. It was a perfect day, with a breeze that carried not only the usual scents of the sea but of the city, too: streets and car exhaust and pretzel stands and oniony salsa and baking bread.

At a turn in the path the wind funneled along the rock and narrowed, bringing together several streams. In this wind she detected Norman's smell again, just a trace. Steve often let her loose for a few minutes at this spot where the trail was quiet and the trees were sparse. Like Norman, he called and whistled her back, but he didn't wait as long, most of the time, and the dynamic was somehow different.

As she ran up through the woods, not really chasing anything – although of course the rabbit dream was still fresh – she was surprised in a wide clearing by a rabbit in the grass ahead, eating clover, unaware of her presence. She drew closer, barked, and the rabbit froze and then dashed away, making a zigzag, leaping across a creek.

With joy and fury she ran, entering freedom. It was a smart, old rabbit, larger than the one in the dream. It disappeared ahead while Carmelita kept running, skirting the creek, slowing down to nose the ground.

It was here that she caught Norman's smell in the air again, stronger than before, a distinctive slice of odor coming through the woods, not just Norman but his house and yard, too. It came strongly, in a clear-cut, redolent shape, so she ran towards it, tracking and triangulating as it appeared and then disappeared. A flash of brown dog through the grass and then the woods, her instincts making innumerable adjustments as she went over the rocky ground, through another grove of trees, pulling away from Steve, having passed beyond the familiar dynamic as the pull of the voice behind her was counteracted by the scent ahead.

It was a matter of chance that Steve had been on the phone with Luisa, talking about the baby, about diapers or formula. On this day the wind was just right and Clementine was fifty or so yards behind a certain boundary line, not ignoring the sound of Steve's voice, distant but clear, calling her name, but overwhelmed by the scent ahead. Simply put, the smell of Norman prevailed over the sound of Steve.

I wish I could make words *be* dog, get into her coat and paws and belly and ears as she ran, slowing down on the main trail, passing the picnic tables, the trash bins, catching now and then the familiar fragrance of home, but also, by this point, her own trace of scent on the asphalt where she had passed a hundred times long ago. If I could make words *be* dog then perhaps I could find the way to inhabit the true dynamic, to imagine a world not defined by notions of power, or morality, or memory, or sentiment, but instead by pure instinct locked in her body, her little legs, as she trotted up the hill along the wall and, when the wall disappeared, cut across manicured grass, past the sign to the park, another great spot to pee, then up the road – staying to the side as she had been taught – to the driveway, stopping there for a moment to sniff.

O ut on the back porch Norman was at a table under a wide, green umbrella, working. Music was coming through the open door. His neck was stiff and he had his hand up and was trying to work out a kink. He sighed and stood to stretch when he heard her bark, once, a big bark for such a small dog. Then he had his arms out and was running and she was running, too, with her body squirming around her flapping tail until he was near and then, with another yip, yip, yip, she was on her back with her belly up, bending this way and that, waiting for his hands, because that was all there was at that moment, his hands lifting her up, lifting, until, still squirming and crying, she was pushing her face into his face, licking and licking as he spoke to her, saying, *Oh girl I missed you so much, I missed you, I let you go and started missing you the second you were gone, and when you were gone I knew I had to go on* and then there was a burst of something beyond the wind itself, beyond the taste of meat, and the two of them were *inside* reunion; even in that moment she was aware that his smell had changed, and she was still dancing on her paws as she went into the house to investigate, checking the floorboard beneath the sink, going from room to room, from one corner to the next.

One day in the fall, keeping the leash tight, he took her back along the path to the spot where she had left him. It might've been that day, or another, when she caught Steve's scent in the wind, the baby, too, and then, another time, Luisa's distinctive scent. In her dreams the rabbit still appeared from time to time, and she ran and leapt and bounded between earth and sky, hovering in bliss and stillness that seemed beyond the animal kingdom. Often, at the end of a long-dreamed chase she met the rabbit and they watched each other from their respective sides of the clearing, frozen inside the moment, speaking with their eyes of the tang of onion grass and the taste of spicy meat. ∎

LABIRINTO

Wiktoria Wojciechowska

Introduction by Lisa Halliday

By any measure, Mussolini's Pontine Marshes project was an impressive logistical feat: five cities built in fewer than ten years on what had been, for millennia, defiantly uninhabitable swampland. Not Caesar, not seven different popes, not even Napoleon had been able to tame the malaria-infested fens; that veterans and laborers mobilized by the Fascists pulled it off, draining and clearing the land so that architects brought in by the regime could erect cities presented as opportunity-rich utopias, elevated Mussolini in many Italians' minds to the status of a beneficent Creator.

'Mussolini Opens Littoria, Extolling Italy's Power,' reported the *New York Times* on 19 December 1934:

> Premier Mussolini today extolled Italy's military power as the guarantee of its agricultural tranquility. He spoke at the inauguration of the country's ninety-third province, Littoria, a farmland reclaimed from the marshes between Rome and Naples.
>
> He said:
> 'Italy must be strong from a military viewpoint so that this gigantic work will not be disturbed. The plow made the furrow, but the sword defends it.'

Littoria, a desolate swampland four years ago, is now occupied by 60,000 former service men and their families. They dwell in modern farmhouses in which they have a proprietary interest.

The cities of Sabaudia, Pontinia, Aprilia and Pomezia opened soon after. Pomezia was inaugurated on 29 October 1939, nearly two months after Germany invaded Poland and only five and a half years before partisans executed Mussolini and his corpse was strung up outside a gas station in Milan. After the war, Littoria was renamed Latina, to play down its Fascist provenance – *Littoria* refers to the lictors, or subordinate officers, who carried the bundles of rods, or fasces, that gave Fascism its name – but even today Littoria is still heard and seen around town, including in the bas-relief of a manhole cover, over a fasces with an axe.

'A marsh extends along the mountain-chain,' wrote Goethe in *Faust*, after visiting the Pontine Marshes in 1787, 'That poisons what so far I've been achieving; / Were I that noisome pool to drain, / 'Twould be the highest, last achieving. / Thus space to many millions I will give / Where, though not safe, yet free and active they may live.'

In 1936, a businessman from New York informed Mussolini that 'the American people would like to know what Fascism is'. 'It is like your New Deal,' Mussolini replied. Indeed, the Fascists put many unemployed Italians back to work building roads, bridges, canals, railway stations, hospitals, orphanages and schools. But the deal they offered was a Faustian one: while you may be active, you won't be free.

Wiktoria Wojciechowska was born in Lublin, Poland, in 1991 and first visited Latina when she was five. Her mother's sister had married an Italian man and moved there. For many years, Latina and its neighboring towns were the only images of Italy Wojciechowska knew; then, in her twenties, she made her first visits to Rome, Naples, Bologna and Venice, and understood that the Pontine Marshes are not your typical Italian destination. Intrigued, she began to research the area online and in Latina's local library. Her aunt had struggled to integrate in the city, and Wojciechowska wondered whether architecture born of a nationalist ideology has the power, decades later, to discourage assimilation, even among those unaware of its history.

Wojciechowska likes to explore places when they are empty. Wandering Latina and the other Pontine Marsh cities during the Italians' siesta, she encountered almost exclusively other non-natives, including refugees from Nigeria, Ghana, Gambia and Mali. In English or French the refugees described feeling stalled, directionless, suspended. Leaving the cities before the immigration officials had made their decision was forbidden, and meanwhile it was difficult to secure work. The migrants did not have much interaction with Italians, and perhaps for this reason were glad to be approached by Wojciechowska, and to be photographed. 'They were sympathetic, proud and fashionable,' Wojciechowska says. 'It was easy and pleasant, as they liked to pose.'

There is irony, of course, in refugees seeking asylum in cities founded on Fascist principles – cities originally conceived for 'pure' Italians and which historians have called a proving ground for the Fascists' attempts to colonize *Africa Italiana*. Today, in Latina, new arrivals must queue for documents at Palazzo M, formerly the Casa del Fascio, an enormous building in the shape of Mussolini's initial. CasaPound, a neo-Fascist faction, has a base in the city, and the region generally supports Italy's right-wing, anti-immigration parties. Locals sympathetic to the migrants include members of a liberal movement called the Sardines, for its mission to pack public squares with demonstrators; there is also Primo Contatto, a collective that aims to facilitate dialogue between Italians and migrants, and many lawyers help asylum seekers for free. Still, a cultish nostalgia for the era of Il Duce abides, and some residents make plain their wish that the migrants would move on. Visiting an association promoting the area's Rationalist architecture, Wojciechowska was informed by the staff who greeted her that foreigners including 'Poles, Ukrainians, Romanians and blacks' were destroying the local landscape. 'The conversation was surreal,' says Wojciechowska, 'as they knew I was Polish.'

Of these photographs, taken between 2017 and 2019, Wojciechowska has said that the emptiness creates an illusion that we are back in the 1930s, before the cities' original inhabitants moved in. She couldn't have known that streets worldwide would soon be empty, evacuated by a crisis more inclusive than any since Fascism called us to war. Now, many of us feel suspended, stalled, involuntarily idle, consigned to an indefinite wait. A pandemic is not an equalizer: we are living as many different versions of this stasis as we lived the unbridled time that preceded it. But still, *this* emptiness, the vanishing of millions for a single microscopic reason, manifests a pact, something closer to unity than many of us have known. In some moments, one takes comfort from this sense of collective purpose: in unity there is strength; the bundle withstands what a single rod cannot. Then one reflects more warily on that image, given the ideology it has been conscripted to serve. The Fascists' notion of racial and ideological purity had a sanitary component, too: Mussolini dreamed of healthy, 'hygienic' cities, free of malaria but also of the filth, crowding, depravation and debauchery he associated with larger, denser, industrial metropolises. The stark, unyielding facades and wide thoroughfares of his Pontine Marshes experiment reflect this asceticism. All but devoid of extrinsic detail, the Fascist aesthetic projects a closed system: unbreachable and immune. But only a city without people is immune. Only a city in which nothing circulates, nothing changes hands, nothing flourishes.

On the internet, Wojciechowska bought some vintage postcards of Latina photographed from the air. With a scalpel, she excised the city's streets, creating a neat labyrinth of negative space, a network of fathomless canals. Her intention was to empty, literally, this maze that detains its subjects, that sends them back to Piazza del Littorio time and again. The initial impression is a kind of blinding, as when someone mutilates a snapshot by cutting out the eyes. But lift the card, lay it on something that isn't pure white, and the effect becomes one of reclamation, renewal. When streets are empty, when venturing into the void even for the permitted reasons feels illicit and fraught, we retreat, inside and inward, where the only escape is metaphysical, along imaginary vectors. With her quiet insurrection, her meticulous surgery on the landscape, the artist has accessed a new axis, another dimension, infinite narratives, a way through. ■

Latina

Pontinia

Latina

Latina

Gibri from Mali, Latina

Latina

Sabaudia

Latina

Clifford from Nigeria, Latina

Latina, known as Littoria between 1932 and 1946

Latina

Pontinia

Sabaudia

Francis from Ghana, Latina

Latina

Pomezia

Latina

Latina

Victor from Nigeria, Latina

Sabaudia

Paul from Nigeria, Latina

Advertisement for Doramad Radioactive Toothpaste

DAUGHTER OF RADIUM

Joe Dunthorne

As a child, my grandmother brushed her teeth every day with radioactive toothpaste. It was called Doramad and the packaging promised a 'wonderful lather' that would reveal 'sparkling, brilliant teeth – radioactive brilliance!' She lived in the small town of Oranienburg, thirty kilometres north of Berlin, where her father was the chemist in charge of making it for the *Auergesellschaft*. Since he was prone to bleeding gums and abscesses, he had also volunteered to be one of Doramad's first test subjects. A colleague had injected his upper gums with Actinium-228 and Radium-228 and for two days his whole mouth had throbbed and swelled but then, suddenly, the inflammation disappeared and the abscess closed. Once Doramad went into commercial production in 1925, he brought tubes of it home to his family. Their third-floor apartment was so close to the factory that, after brushing her teeth at night, my grandmother would lie in bed and listen to the churning of the autoclave.

On the morning my wife and I arrive in Oranienburg, ninety-four years later, the local authorities are draining the river. A 500-kilo bomb has been found buried in the soft banks of the Havel and they are lowering the water level to reach it. It is a big operation; a row of pipes like a church organ slurp at the muddy water. Five thousand people are being evacuated from their homes while a hundred police and firefighters establish the perimeter. This is the 209th bomb from the Second World War to be found in this town since German unification in 1990 and authorities estimate that as many as 400 remain beneath the ground. That's one for every hundred residents.

Most of the bombs have chemical fuses that were supposed to delay detonation by a few hours or days but ended up working to a schedule of decades. Whether it's now or fifty years from now, they will all go off eventually. In November 2013, Gunthard 'Paule' Dietrich returned from walking his dog to find his home was gone and in its place a twenty-metre crater was pooling with brown water. The authorities had hoped to defuse the bomb buried in his garden but, in the end, saw no choice but to detonate. The man in charge was André 'the Blast Master' Müller, the head of the Oranienburg bomb squad. He is something of a local celebrity. With his pot belly, grey moustache and zip-up fleece, he resembles an off-season Poirot. Along with Mr Dietrich, he is one of the stars of *The Bomb Hunters*, a documentary about life in 'the most dangerous town in Germany'.

We walk north, away from the cordon, towards the local archive. It is housed in a former stately home – one of the few noteworthy buildings to have survived the Second World War – and there we meet the archivist, Christian Becker. We are hoping that he can help us find out about my family – my grandmother, Dorothea, her brother and her parents – who lived in Oranienburg until 1935 when, as Jews, they fled to Turkey. They left behind much of their money and their belongings and it was only during the 1936 Olympics, when they hoped that the presence of the world's press would limit Nazi aggression, that they decided to return to Berlin and Oranienburg in order to conduct a heist on their own home.

Christian has a colourful silk scarf wrapped round his neck. For someone who has spent twenty-one years attending to a basement archive which details Oranienburg's role in one of the darkest periods of human history, he is surprisingly chipper. When he sees us, he expresses surprise that we are 'so young'. We sense this says more about his usual clientele than it does about our youthfulness.

Leading us down into the low-ceilinged basement, Christian talks about the bomb in the river as we might talk about the weather. He tells us that whenever there's an evacuation, the kids are disappointed if they don't get a day off school. He explains that Oranienburg is the only town in Germany that is actively searching for unexploded bombs. And every few weeks, they find one.

The Allies had many good reasons to target Oranienburg. Military aircraft were built here, there was a laboratory to develop new chemical weapons and a factory that made gas masks, including the 'J' filters that the SS used when operating the gas chambers. In 1933, one of Germany's first concentration camps – largely for political prisoners – was opened in an old brewery in the centre of town. In 1936, a bigger second camp, Sachsenhausen, was built on the northern edge of Oranienburg. Two hundred thousand people were interred there; 100,000 died. From 1940, a secret facility produced one tonne of uranium oxide each month as part of the Nazis' attempts to develop nuclear weapons. In 2017, a local metal detectorist happened across a rock with unusual properties and took it home to show his children. Two days later, his street was evacuated while government workers took away the radioactive lump in a lead-lined suitcase. In other words, Oranienburg is the town where Berlin hid its secrets.

In the context of all this, my great-grandfather's involvement in Doramad toothpaste seems almost quaint until Christian explains where the radioactive ingredients ended up. The thorium used to make the toothpaste was extracted from radioactive monazite sand which had been imported from Brazil. Huge piles of it lay around the grounds of the factory. When the people of Oranienburg started to rebuild the town after the war, they filled the bomb craters with whatever material was readily available. In this way, the foundations of Oranienburg are now both radioactive and explosive. It is not unusual for André Müller and his team to wear hazmat suits while they dig.

Disappearing into the rows of shelves, Christian finds a directory of postal addresses from 1931–2 and is pleased to discover my great-grandfather's name, Siegfried Merzbacher. He and his wife Lilli lived at Lindenstraße 15. Before I can ask whether that building still exists, Christian shows us a large poster pinned to the wall: a composite of aerial photos of Oranienburg taken by the American and British bombers after the huge raid on 15 March 1945, when over 4,000 bombs were dropped in forty-five minutes. Oranienburg is a moonscape. These aerial photos are what André Müller and his team use as a map in their attempts to locate the remaining live explosives. Craters show where bombs went off and smaller keyhole dots indicate where they didn't – and where they might still be buried. Christian points his finger at a rash of craters and says, 'Here's Lindenstraße.'

I shelve my hopes of ever standing in my grandmother's childhood bedroom. On the upside, however, Christian does find a box file that contains the architectural plan of their apartment. They lived in a building that was built and owned by Auer, my great-grandfather's employers, a company that had made its name selling a mildly radioactive gas lamp – the Auerlicht – before diversifying into toothpaste, gas masks and radioluminescent paint. Christian unfolds the crumbly pages, revealing a grand three-storey corner building with a steep red-tiled roof, high windows and a panelled front door flanked by columns. A vertical section shows the inside of the building. I peer into the attic and wonder if that's where they hid the jewellery box that contained the bloodstone ring that I'm now wearing. It's a story I first heard from my mother when she gave it to me, how this was one of the items my family smuggled out of Nazi Germany in 1936.

She never gave me any more detail than that and yet I've been retelling the story ever since, making it more dramatic each time I do, so that now Siegfried's palms are slippery on the wheel as they head south through Berlin in the middle of the Olympics, past sports fans with flags around their shoulders, past huge swastikas lining the Lustgarten, storm troopers on every corner – his driving becoming suddenly self-conscious, taking each turn with elaborate care – and it is only many hours later – as Jesse Owens, an African American sprinter, breaks the world 100-metre record while the Führer looks on, seething – that Siegfried Merzbacher, portly Jewish chemist with his kids in the back and an unusually heavy briefcase, is waved across the border into Czechoslovakia.

Christian returns with another box file. He has discovered that there was also an air-raid shelter in the basement of the building, installed in 1932. This is surprising, he explains, because typically air-raid shelters were not built in Germany until 1938 or later. We ask why they would have singled out the residents of this building for special protection but, for the first time today, Christian does not have an answer.

When we get back outside, a siren sounds. Minutes later, the protective cordon is lowered and residents return to their homes. Photos on social media show André Müller with his hand resting proudly on another disarmed American bomb. It is orange with rust and resembles a whole roast pig, an oilcloth stuffed in its mouth. We watch the mayor hand Müller supermarket flowers and thank him because there is now 'one less monster in Oranienburg'. Only 400 monsters to go.

W alking through the quiet, wide streets, we try not to think about the homes built on radioactive sand, the lumps of uranium found lying in the long grass or the unexploded bombs beneath our feet, nose up. It probably doesn't help that my wife is pregnant. Next week we'll be going for our 'anomaly scan'. We envisage the doctor asking, 'So remind me why you spent a long weekend in Germany's most radioactive town?'

At the edge of a football pitch, a small grey sign explains that Auer built extra factories here to meet the increased demand for gas masks as the country prepared for war. Then, from 1943 to 1945, the factory buildings were taken over to extend the Sachsenhausen concentration camp. Where we are now standing, as many as 2,000 female prisoners lived in barracks, forced to make masks that would be used to protect the SS while they operated the gas chambers. On 15 March 1945 – the day thousands of bombs fell on Oranienburg – hundreds of these prisoners were killed. They had no air-raid shelters. We look up from reading the sign to see young footballers in tracksuits doing shuttle runs, weaving between cones, their breath huffing in the cold. Beyond them, steam rises from a sports complex: swimming pool, sauna and wellness centre.

A few minutes' walk away, we find an astroturfed playing field that was once the cobbled playground of my grandmother's old primary school. The school has changed names since she was here but it remains on the same site. In 1933, when she was nine years old, a new law limited the number of Jewish children in each school to 1.5 per cent of the total intake. Since she was already the only Jewish child in her class, life continued as normal for her. Nevertheless, the school's director, Professor Katz, went out of his way to promise her that she would be treated no differently to any other child. At that time, Professor Katz was still flying the black, red and gold flag of the Weimar Republic above the school, telling the parent–teacher association that he would not withdraw it at the request of 'any association of goatherds'. A few weeks later, a group of those goatherds arrived at the school in SS uniforms, burned the flag and raised the swastika. From then on, each morning, Dorothea stood in silence while her fellow students saluted the Führer and sang anti-Semitic songs. She told me that on occasion she found herself singing along with some of the less offensive ones, 'but only because the tunes were good'.

Their apartment was just around the corner from the school, at the junction of Lindenstraße and Lehnitzstraße. On one side of the road – where the toothpaste factory was – is now a Park & Ride car park. On the other side, where the apartment stood, there are bland, prefabricated blocks built in the 1960s when Oranienburg was part of East Germany. Between two of these buildings, we notice a fenced-off area that looks like an ordinary construction site. Then we see the rows of regularly spaced bore holes that mean the bomb squad have been here, digging.

While peering through, we do some research on our phones. My wife learns that Oranienburg remains a popular weekend destination for the amateur radiation spectrometrist community. They like it for the soil samples. I discover a survey by the Federal Office for Radiation Protection from 1997. As well as highlighting the places where bomb craters were filled with monazite sand, it picks out three areas with greatly increased radioactivity in Oranienburg. The first is on the canal at the edge of town. The second is where we've just been, the football pitches and sports centre. The third is where we are right now.

Without a word, we start walking back to the train station.

That evening, in a vaulted room within the huge onion-shaped dome of Berlin's central synagogue, we stand to have our picture taken beside a life-size image of my late grandmother. She's part of an exhibition about former refugees who, from 1969 onwards, returned to Berlin at the invitation of the city, to see how much it had changed and to tell their story to younger generations. At the height of the programme in 1987, Berlin's Senate chartered planes and flew nearly 2,000 former refugees from as far away as New York, Buenos Aires and Tokyo. The survivors were greeted with roses on the runway at Tegel. Naturally, the numbers are dwindling now and the city authorities no longer charter flights. Last year, there were fewer than a hundred guests. Soon there won't be any.

'And then what?' Martina Voigt, the curator of the exhibition, asks. 'What will happen when there's nobody left to tell this story?' One could argue that question has already been answered, in part, by the 2016 state elections, when 14.1 per cent of Berliners voted for the far-right, anti-immigration party Alternative für Deutschland. This presents a problem for Martina. When former refugees return to the city of their youth, she wants them to see how different it is now. And usually, she says, they get a good impression of Berlin. In fact, she has 'searched hard for any bad experiences and found none'. And yet she feels concerned. She shows us a poem written by one of the returning refugees. He praises the city that Berlin has become, how 'nobody gives orders or barks' any more. There's a long silence and then her voice cracks as she speaks: 'But he's wrong. We just made sure he didn't meet those people.'

B ack home, I begin a search for the mythical document that only the most underemployed of my close relatives have managed to read: my great-grandfather's memoir. It is comprised of nearly 2,000 pages of unpublished typescript, in German, which he started writing in 1961 while living in North Carolina. When I ask my parents about it, they are not sure where it is. Maybe in a chest of drawers in my grandmother's cottage in the Scottish Borders? Maybe in the Jewish Museum in Berlin? Of my immediate family, the only person who has read it is my father. He is a historian, specialising in seventeenth-century Holland, and so when he says he found it 'a bit of a slog', I know I'm in trouble.

Siegfried wrote his memoir in the last nine years of his life and he was still adding footnotes to it when he died in 1970. The substantially abridged English translation, which is all I find at my grandmother's cottage, was completed forty-two years later, by my great-uncle, aged ninety-two, while he was living in a retirement home. He died just days after finishing it. Holding this ring-bound document in both hands, I am aware that it was an end-of-life project for two generations of my family.

Across hundreds of thousands of words, Siegfried manages to say almost nothing about their first-hand experience of the Third Reich. The memoir 'officially' ends on the day Hitler came to power. Much of the book details our ancestral history, starting with Jizhak Merzbacher, an eighteenth-century trader of animal hides from north-east Bavaria. The manuscript also spends a great deal of time on Siegfried's grandmother, Nanny Merzbacher, including a hundred pages of her diary which he faithfully typed up, word for word. In the English translation, her daily life was deemed insufficiently interesting and the diary was cut in its entirety, though we do still get a sense of

Nanny's character, how she 'had a sharp tongue and left no good hair on anyone . . . including herself', a quality that survived undiluted in my own grandmother, Dorothea.

When Siegfried does reflect on his life in Oranienburg, raising a family in the shadow of fascism, one of his frustrating tics is that he typically follows difficult episodes with soothing memories of a holiday. No sooner has he recalled a train journey to Berlin in early 1933, when he was 'too cowardly' to intervene as a storm trooper dragged a 'polite and quiet' Jewish-looking gentleman out of the carriage, than he is drawn back to 1893, aged ten, travelling with his family to the coast at Blankenberge where he saw – for the first time – the 'infinite extension' of the sea. If a single sentence could define the whole book, it would be: 'From this unpleasant subject I now return to my childhood vacations.'

In July 1930, the yard behind Siegfried's factory was stacked high with fragrant piles of prune and peach stones, coconut and almond shells, raw materials for the production of activated charcoal, a substance which could trap and neutralise poison gases. Siegfried had just accepted a promotion at Auer, moving from toothpaste to the role of supervisor in the 'protection' division. This meant he was in charge of producing and testing charcoal filters in gas masks. Day and night, his assistants fed the peach stones and coconut shells into a rotating furnace and, for the first time in his twenty-three-year-long career, Siegfried felt he was doing something valuable.

For the most part, testing the filters against poison gas could be done in the relative safety of the laboratory, with a step photometer and an exhaust hood. Nevertheless, it was sometimes deemed necessary for the chemists to undertake more dangerous field tests. In his first week, he'd watched a young colleague succumb to nitrogen narcosis. Wearing a full-face mask, Dr Fries had run in wild circles round the ice cellar before dropping to the flagstones. Siegfried thought he was dead but, when they pulled the mask off, he sat up as though waking from a nap.

As the division's new supervisor, Siegfried felt there was pressure on him to show willing – which was why he found himself sitting on a bench in an airtight tank while three colleagues peered in through a window of inch-thick glass. The air he was breathing contained 4,000 parts of CO_2 per million, roughly ten times the density you would expect in the air outside, yet still far below the level of oxygen deprivation. Presuming he breathed normally, which he was trying to do, then he should feel no more uncomfortable than he would in a stuffy meeting room. He and his colleagues were also studying how humidity interacts with CO_2 and he could feel the wall-mounted humidifier breathing on his neck. He should have told his colleagues that he was prone to bouts of light-headedness – had fainted once while climbing the stairs to his apartment – but he didn't want to seem feeble. He looked out at the faces of his new colleagues: Herr Otte, Herr Worbs and Dr Puetter. He could see their mouths moving but couldn't hear them.

He opened the pad on his lap and, with his pencil, made notes in Gabelsberger, an elegant shorthand. The atmosphere in the tank was close and tasted faintly acidic but he felt fine. Forty minutes later, he made another note, acknowledging the headache that was now grinding behind his eyeballs. Closing his eyes for a moment, he thought about his daughter and his son. What was more irresponsible: to agree to be gently gassed, or to refuse to take part and perhaps put his job at risk? He was always conscious of stereotypes about Jews that he felt he needed to disprove. It had been the same during the war. People said that Jews got all the cushy non-combat roles, the office jobs, and sent everyone else to choke to death on the front line. As soon as he heard that rumour, he immediately reported to his superiors and asked to be sent into the field. He remembers a long moment of silence before First Lieutenant Voelker calmly pointed out that what really mattered was finding the role that best suited the skills of each individual and, in his case, that would be secretarial work. Voelker managed to say this without sounding patronising, but that didn't stop Siegfried from feeling judged. And that night in the barracks with the other reserves, when Siegfried fell asleep on his inflatable pillow, his comrades deflated it.

He looked out at his colleagues, tried to read their lips as they spoke. He felt that most of them were good people. Herr Otte was, like him, a committed Social Democrat and they occasionally met at meetings of the Schwarz-Rot-Gold. Herr Worbs was certainly a liberal, if not card-carrying. Dr Puetter he was less sure about. He treated Siegfried like a subordinate.

After more than two hours, Siegfried rocked his feet back and forth as they started to prickle. He made a note of it in his pad and, looking down, saw that his Gabelsberger had become involuntarily italicised. He stamped his feet to try and get the feeling back. All three colleagues were watching him now, their faces at the glass. In Herr Worb's narrowing eyes he noted genuine concern; Herr Otte's breath misted the glass and he wiped it away with the sleeve of his lab coat; Dr Puetter's expression remained disconcertingly professional. Siegfried's pencil clattered to the floor. When he leaned down to pick it up, his vision swam. A moment later he was sitting on the ground. He looked up at his colleagues and they looked down at him.

Siegfried was not asked to be a test subject again – nor did he volunteer. From then on, he focused on testing the gas mask filters in laboratory conditions. This was also dangerous work, but at least he was in control. The masks had to meet strict military standards, a fact that he was reminded of each morning when Dr Engelhard arrived from Auer's head office in Berlin. Dr Engelhard feigned the air of an academic – and liked to mention that he lectured at the Technical University in Berlin – but Siegfried knew he was a military man. In the field of chemical weapons, he was interested in everything except chemistry. Still, Siegfried had a grudging respect for him since Dr Engelhard had worked under Fritz Haber, the German-Jewish chemist who could have turned the war for Germany, had the military generals believed him when he said his new weapon – mustard gas – would be ruthlessly effective. Haber was one of Siegfried's heroes: a Nobel Prize-winning chemist, German first and Jewish second.

Auer continued to shift their focus towards military contracts and in 1931 they opened what was called a Gas Protection School in Oranienburg. This was the reason why, by 1932, Siegfried's apartment building had its own air-raid shelter in the basement. The Gas Protection School was run by one of Siegfried's colleagues, Karl Wollin, a Jewish chemist, and the idea was to educate the military, fire departments and coal mining industries about poisonous gases, the proper use of gas masks and preparation for firebomb and gas attacks. Every week, Herr Wollin would bring groups of men to the apartment building. He would show them the importance of removing flammable objects from the roof space and take them down to the air-raid shelter to run through disaster scenarios.

My grandmother couldn't wait to try out the shelter for herself. On weekends, she and her brother would sneak inside and role-play the town's destruction. When Herr Wollin heard about their enthusiasm, he asked the Merzbachers if they would let their children be photographed in the shelter. This was just the kind of image that would lighten the sometimes too-ominous tone of the Gas Protection School's monthly magazine, *The Gas Mask*. Though the idea made Siegfried and Lilli uncomfortable, they didn't want to be uncooperative, and the photograph was taken and published. It featured all the children in the apartment building standing in the shelter. Eugen, my great-uncle, aged ten at the time, is happily cranking the ventilator.

Over the following years, the gas school moved steadily away from 'protection' and, by 1942, it was training the SS in how to use 'disinfectants', most notably Zyklon B. Officially, the school taught them only how to 'delouse' clothes and tackle pest 'infestations'; in reality, they learned how to use a newly commissioned variant of Zyklon B that was not intended as a pesticide. This version contained no 'warning agent', the pungent chemical that caused retching and vomiting, and which was originally designed to save lives by making it nearly impossible for humans to stay in a room that had been recently fumigated. The removal of the warning agent made the substance far more dangerous to use and there was only one context in which this had advantages. Whether it was an act of mercy – an attempt to make deaths more painless – or merely pragmatism – because the residual smell of the additive would have warned the victims of their fate – it is clear that the 'disinfectors' of Oranienburg were learning how to kill humans.

If Siegfried knew about this later development in the Gas Protection School, he doesn't mention it in his memoir. While occasional details of what happened after 1933 emerge through footnotes and momentary digressions, even these tend to be oddly cheerful. At one point, Siegfried interrupts a reverie about his childhood artistic experiences – how he 'totally fail[ed] to appreciate classical music' – and mentions the first time he took his children to the opera, a wonderful performance of Engelbert Humperdinck's *Hänsel und Gretel* that they saw in Berlin. It was the summer of 1936.

While Siegfried's memoir offers little else on this period, I have more luck when listening to interviews with my grandmother. There are four hours in German with the Anne Frank museum, a documentary by BBC Radio Scotland, footage from a project called *Refugee Voices* and an audio recording that was never released. She rarely enjoyed being interviewed but, in this last one, she sounds particularly sour. The interviewer's questions keep circling 1936, their trip back to Germany and the heist on their home. Did they feel threatened? How much had Germany changed? Did they witness any anti-Semitism? Was she scared? Could she offer more specifics? She recognises the tone of someone digging for trauma. Her yawns become audible and aggressive and eventually she says, 'Look, why don't you just read a book about it?'

Her mean streak was usually leavened with humour: as a German-Jewish Scot, she could flash from bluntness to comedy and back to bluntness. But at the end of her life, she eased up on the comedy and, in her final years, she burned through NHS carers at the rate of one a week.

In the interview, she exhales loudly, then finally proceeds to give more details about their departure from Oranienburg. She explains that, while his Jewishness prevented him from working for Auer in Germany, he still remained one of their overseas employees. In 1935, the company helped to arrange transport and a visa for Turkey. They set him up with a new job in Ankara, establishing their new gas mask factory. She remembers leaving on the luxurious Orient Express: 'two days and nights of eating'. She talks about travelling back to Germany in August 1936 and staying for a full five weeks. There was no heist. Her parents bought her a new violin. Her brother was given a brand-new Leica camera. They both had regular French lessons with a teacher who opened the door each day and said: 'Children, would you like a pretzel?' They visited relatives in Munich and Berlin, and the story starts to sound like a summer holiday. When the interviewer says he has no more questions, her chair scrapes back and she says, 'Oh thank God.'

What makes listening to all this even worse is that the interviewer is me. It was conducted ten years ago, when I first tried to write about my family's history. By any professional standards, it is a disaster. The recording begins with my grandmother halfway through an anecdote while I audibly fumble with the dictaphone. '*Sorry*,' I say, interrupting, 'I realised it wasn't on. Who . . . who . . . who committed suicide?' It doesn't get much better after that.

I remember giving up on the whole project because, as I saw it, I hadn't been able to find enough details. I realise now that there were plenty of details – just not the ones I liked.

Two weeks after returning from Oranienburg, I receive news that the exhibition featuring my grandmother is being transferred to the House of Representatives, Berlin's state parliament. This is where Alternative für Deutschland won 14.1 per cent of the seats. Before the election, Berlin's mayor, Michael Müller, said that if the AfD got double figures it would be 'seen around the world as a sign of the return of the right wing and the Nazis in Germany'.

Martina asks if I will speak at the opening ceremony, talk about our family history for ten minutes, which feels not nearly long enough for the messy truth. Over the next few weeks, I make various failed attempts to write the speech. I keep wondering if it's a good idea – in a building housing the resurgent far right in Germany – to describe how my family was helped to emigrate by a company who trained the SS to operate the gas chambers, how they cruised out of the Third Reich on the Orient Express, then came back to Berlin a year later to buy presents and see the opera.

I am saved from this decision by the news that the exhibition has been cancelled. Though the coronavirus has not yet reached Germany, government guidance recommends against any large gatherings: bringing together in one room a group of the few surviving Jewish refugees, all of whom are over eighty, seems particularly inadvisable.

My appointment with the Jewish Museum is also cancelled. They have the full, unedited typescript of Siegfried's memoir, as well as his private correspondence and diaries, all the details he chose to leave out.

M y grandmother was ninety-three when she died. As people often do in the last years of their life, she returned more and more to her childhood. Even though she'd lived in Scotland for fifty years, she said she no longer belonged there. She started speaking German again. She even got a new German boyfriend, Ernst. They met at a get-together for Jewish refugees in Scotland and were both glad to find someone with whom they could speak their native language. Every time the phone rang, her eyes lit up: 'Oh, that'll be my man.' They spent hours chatting each night, like teenagers.

She started saying that she and Ernst were going to drive down to Marseille together, see the Mediterranean. Considering that she'd long ago become a risk to other road users and stopped driving – that she hadn't left Edinburgh in over a year – this was quite a plan. But the carers advised us not to contradict her. At this point, facts cease to matter. So we went with the story she wanted to tell, let her pack a small suitcase, agreed that she would soon be at the wheel, her boyfriend reclining beside her, blazing down a road carved into the mountainside, steering them south until it rises into view, the infinite extension of the sea. ■

It felt like they were going to ride it out, for all the catalogue of what they'd done; that they'd surf a national wave of commingled anxiety and goodwill and hope and fear and uncertainty and all the rest, and that those venting and disbelieving would be *politicising a tragedy* when *now was not the time.* We were all in shock, angry or not. This was the early days, when Johnson was reciting *Boy's Own* blather – we will *take it on the chin*, we will *send coronavirus packing*, and, oh look, it turns out that even in the midst of everything else you can still roll your eyes and cringe. Followed instantly by the shame of the mark: it's not as if provoking *bien-pensant* embarrassment isn't also the point of Johnson's Churchill-as-farce. He's goading the goadable no less than pleasing the easily pleased. But knowing you're being grifted doesn't make you immune to it. Back in the dully glowing Coronaviral Bronze Age we were All In It Together. The ironclad rule: any time any politician deploys the first-person plural, start asking what kind of bullshit you are being fed.

When Covid-19 struck Johnson, not content with obligatorily wishing him a speedy recovery, some Labour politicians tweet-simpered a gratitude profoundly undeserved. ('Thank you for everything your Government is doing to help us fight this': Sadiq Khan. '[T]hanks for what you have been doing to help the country fight this': Andy Burnham.) You certainly didn't have to be one of the edgelords publicly wishing Johnson death to find this – to a PM who'd recently decreed that pubs could stay open but that you shouldn't go, who'd boasted of still shaking patients' hands, who'd floated a version of 'herd immunity', who'd allowed racing and football matches and concerts to continue after his own advisers called for lockdown, who'd dispensed with track-and-trace, who'd failed to follow up offers to help with ventilator production, and on and on and on – a grotesque dereliction of opposition.

An early epoch of discombobulation, frantic mass stats-crunching, the boning-up on reproduction numbers and beginners' guides to epidemiology. Of rummaging through cupboards and learning what you didn't have. You grew familiar with the feel of a meat thermometer's spike under the tongue. With the sight of new rejectamenta; blue skintight gloves like husks shed mid-crawl. Still you couldn't but live like something suspended, watching from behind glass, sensing an approach.

They governed by truculent hint and pre-haunt: we may have to lock down, we may have to extend and tighten this, we rule nothing out, training us to know what that meant: prepare yourselves. Not that this was willing. 'We didn't want to go down this route in the first place – public and media pressure pushed the lockdown,' kvetched some high-ranked source to the *Telegraph*. Because of the economy, stupid – the baleful effects on which are, yes, incalculable, an epochal shock. But this resistance is economically illiterate in its own terms, a symptom of decades of worshipping rentier accumulation. And, in the face of mass death, it's turpitude. These 'hawks' are more clubbable cousins of the deranged *morituri* for neoliberalism, the initiates of outlier cults who are insistent not that risks are not real but that it's *dulce et decorum* to be ready to die for the dollar. Hayek's 'party of life' needs its Valkyries, its suicide squads.

Their piacular dreams move them to strange poetries, inverted vatic insight. 'While death is sad for the living left behind,' writes Bill Mitchell, one Trumpian provocateur demanding the end of lockdown, 'for the dying, it is merely a passage out of this physical body to a spiritual existence, free of this mortal coil.' This is why we should have no fear. 'If one turns off the radio, the music is still there. For all we know, the dead weep for us.'

At last the scandals piled up enough, and the British press decreed with its bystander ingenuousness that the administration was 'on the defensive'.

These moments are always weird and contradictory. The government's approval ratings remain higher than they've been in years, even as national rage grows, in this moment of uncanny suspension, of watching, like specimens in formalin, staring out in the long light at unspeakably beautiful planeless skies, breathing cleaner air and hearing giddily bickering animals, and your held breath feels as if it might emerge as a shout. You laugh too long and hard, your temper's short, your tongue feels thick in your mouth.

People who've overseen a years-long spiralling crisis in the NHS put rainbow images in their windows, stand on their doorsteps and #clapforcarers every Thursday with shit-eating grins. At least now there's a growing sense that they should go fuck themselves. 'We do not have any basic surgical masks,' Dr Peter Tun wrote desperately to his managers. 'We do not have eye protection kits, gowns nor scrubs.' If they were not given such equipment soon, 'it will be too little and too late'. Two weeks after he wrote that he was diagnosed with the disease. A week later he died. Every Thursday, the Cabinet claps as if the blood on their hands won't spatter.

There are those who swear by hot water, disinfectant, certain foods. For whom the 5G mast is the new Air Loom, sowing sickness. There's a species of left condescension for which such fallacies are opiates of the oppressed, deflections of just class rage. That's sociologically simplistic. What's harder to contest is the intuition that governmental claims to have matters in hand and our best interests at heart are worth a bowl of piss. And more condescending still is the lumpen rationalist, railing against tinfoil hats and the motes in other people's eyes. Our era is one of agnatology and nostrum-collapse: superstitions and talismanic thinking proliferate. The mesmeric hoodoo 'fluence of Russian bots; the transformative powers of impeachment; the fundamental decent klutziness of our rulers, who might cock up but would never conspire: the conspiracy-scolds, too, have their lullabies.

And they have their shibboleths. A celebrated author spits righteous fire about the parlous state of the nation. Saves his hottest flames for the end: if the government, 'for Brexit-related reasons', failed to collect as much PPE as possible via an EU scheme, the front bench should face charges of conspiracy to murder. What of all those manifold other scandals, *non*-Brexit-related decisions and evasions that have led to deaths? Are they not also evidence for the prosecution?

At least it is a piece about the world. At least it's angry. What is this self-flagellating urge to read all the lockdown diaries, all the 'Not another lockdown diary!' first lines? These reams of writerly vacuities, column after *mot juste*-hunting column describing this shape of the day, this view from the window, such-and-such a tree and such, this which is on the desk, this which is in the fridge what with food not being as easy to get these days, these the new modes of going to the shops, this which is the conversation that was had with this friend or child or neighbour, this, now you mention it, which is the newly warm neighbourly discourse, this the recourse to Netflix, this the thing the author had thought they would miss and does not, this the one they weren't expecting to and do. This the sense that things will never be the same again. Et cetera, repeat to fade. They provoke incredulousness greater than the sky. Who gives a fuck?

In the city, amid the tragedy and trauma, we're granted a new silence. Distinct. Not total, any more than what we used to think of as London quiet, in the minutes between cars at night, the sound of a distant train part of the silence itself. Now you can hear the wings of a bird you watch. And when a car or van or a delivery driver on a scooter – one of the new heroes – passes by, the interruption startles. Glimpsing home-exercisers through windows you're overwhelmed with affection for a new sort of community. Mist comes and goes across your vision: your mask sends breath on to your glasses. What would this lockdown be if it were autumn? What if it were winter?

At the close of the eighties, Helen Chadwick created her *Viral Landscapes*, images of paint-smeared canvases attached to great panoramic photographs of the Pembrokeshire coast overlayed with blown-up images of cells from her mouth, ear, cervix, kidney, blood. Wilderness, through the stained-glass window of the body. 'The living integrates with other in an infinite continuity of matter and welcomes difference not as damage but as potential,' Chadwick said.

Less than a decade later she died, terribly young. A heart attack, perhaps linked to a viral infection.

Look out across the roofs and those images recur, now that we know we live in a viral landscape. Whatever the aftermath, you won't see the city again except through the agency of absence, recalling this semi-emptiness, this viral uncertainty. Only key workers – a newly vital category of the recently undervalued – are tested. Even those of us knocked down for weeks by illness can't know without all doubt if we've had it, or know if we can still pass it on. Care means leaving space, and in these bright warm days the city is full of spaces. Thus, in negative, Chadwick's self, integrated with the other.

A photograph of an American demonstrator of Bill Mitchellian ilk does the rounds: on their placard, SOCIAL DISTANCING = COMMUNISM. Would that it were so.

Store up descriptions for a curious future. As well as everything else that this is – an experiment, a contested machine of petty spites and of astonishing kindness and solidarity – the new city is a found artwork, and a rumination on itself.

For Fredric Jameson, urban absence is key to a modernist imaginary, the vacant city 'revealing an object world forever suspended on the brink of meaning, forever disposed to receive a revelation of evil or of grace that never comes. The unpeopled streets, the oppressive silence, convey this absent presence like a word on the tip of your tongue or a dream not quite remembered.' These streets are depleted but not empty, and the silence is anything but oppressive. For all that, in the viral city there is such a sense of endlessly receding meaning. Everything is vivid, pregnant, a receptacle eager to be filled with meaning, with something, and if the revelation has not yet come there is a growing intimation, one that we must cultivate, that this absence is an invitation. We have not been passed by: this is an opportunity.

The historical odds suggest that when whatever comes, comes, it will be evil. But we don't have to sit back and take that. We might have something to say about it.

These are days of viral anger and despair and fear but of something else, too.

'We will miss this when it's over,' she says to you.

Somewhere among all that is evoked by all the death, the suffering, the brutal, disproportionate impact on BAME people, the unspeakable conditions of those at the sharp edges of danger; on those locked in with terrorising partners in shitty flats much too small, on renters still unprotected, on all those terrified of destitution, without support, without resources, you blinked, felt guilt, at the rising of a certain excitement. A breathlessness. That after so many years of feeling that some Event was due, that something vast must surely happen, something vast happened. Is happening.

Of all the various investigations of our Covid state, probably the most important, certainly the most moving, came in mid-April, from a YouGov poll for the Royal Society of Arts' Food, Farming and Countryside commission. Citing the air, the wildlife, closer social bonds and other factors, 85 per cent of those questioned said they want to retain at least some of the changes wrought by these moments. Fewer than one in ten desire to return to the status quo ante.

Even with all there is behind them, we find value in these days. What a wrenching thing. That in this we glimpse something new, something we want, a viral landscape we deserve. ∎

Communion

Rachel Long

after Deana Lawson

Behold the miracle of afro hair.
Blackness so complete
you could put your hand in
never get it back. Recognise
the shark eyes of boredom,
the dial of two women
tending to every hair on your head
cussing a curve into a needle,
thick thread spooling,
the scissors are just there
but teeth are closer.
Ever sat for thirteen hours
in the same chair?
Scalp sliced so many times
you can't recall if you are girl
or railroad?
Ever not received what was meant to be
in the bag? – Softness, *Whappened?*
Ain't never seen no half-white hair like this!
Choose a new version of yourself
every 2–3 months. Be Russian, Hawaiian,
Virgin – at 10, 16,
22 inches. Go electric blue, blonde,
Faith Evans-auburn.
Enter the shabby palaces
named after the high priestesses;
En Vogue, Cleopatra, Rihanna;

promising next to nothing –
not an appointment, good service,
politeness, a mirror,
that you'll leave before dark;
to be left with half a head
so another customer can be squeezed in
for Ghana braids, you're kidding
if you think that a box of wings and chips
won't be eaten over your fresh weave,
leftover finger-grease used to smooth it.
Lord grant me serenity and deliver me
from the *Titanic* song by Celine Dion
on everlasting pull-up,
radio warbling atop wet towels,
but it's either Celine's heart going on and on
and on, or the cacophony of phone calls
about papers, Pampers, the dance tonight-tonight.
Girl, you're the blackest you might ever be in here,
stop pulling away
from the crepe roll of her belly
over tightest jeans. Let it rise,
rest on your earlobe.
Dare to breathe regular on her hand;
Jackie, Marcia, Tat, omnipresent aunties
who don't flinch or say you breathe too heavy.
When you are finally did,
you tip, she pockets it, saying,
dese little white pickney dem
always have money.

Mourning Dove, Winter from 'Natura Morta' series, 1992

HOW THINGS END

Ann Beattie

As I began to flip through a literary magazine, I was stopped by a photograph of myself as a young girl, standing beside my college professor. I was wearing a striped bathing suit with a shirt thrown over it; he was in cutoffs, a long wad of string dangling down one leg. If I'd ever seen the picture, I'd forgotten it. Beside me stood Gomer, in his big, aviator-style glasses, who, in his thirties, had reemerged in my life, having renamed himself Grover. After he'd dropped out of graduate school, following a disastrous affair with a fellow graduate student in his biology lab (she also left and returned to Korea), Grover – which still sounds to me like the name of a dog – had a heart-to-heart with me and confessed his undying love. When I expressed little enthusiasm, he turned bitter. Not in the moment. When he said this to me, we were finishing lunch at a sidewalk cafe in New York, where I was working as an office temp. The waitress had been flirting with him by bringing more of the good bread and whisking away the basket of untouched, anemic-looking rolls. By then, he'd become almost handsome. He wore contact lenses, and he'd found a way to stop wincing when he made dismissive motions with his hands. As my father would have said, he'd grown into his looks. His nose was proportionate to his face; his hair, longer. And his generally improved demeanor meant that his eyebrows no longer nearly converged at the bridge of his nose, making the listener assume he'd been skeptical of every word that had been said. He'd enrolled in a very competitive (three tries, many recommendations) acting program in Greenwich Village. So when he stated his feelings about me, had he been acting? As we split the check, I'd found myself wondering if everything he'd said had been an elaborate put-on, or perhaps, in some odd way, a put-down. Otherwise, how could I have felt so diminished?

The photograph was an illustration of a long essay. I could see small children in the background, playing on rocks mostly submerged in water, and remembered that Gomer, *Grover*, had at some point felt one of them was in danger, and had risen to approach the little group, only to be set upon by an enormous woman, who appeared from nowhere, like a bird of prey, and who kept insisting that everything was under control. Where had she come from? She could have been anybody, though no doubt she was someone's mother. We'd let her contend with a wailing child's cut foot, forcing ourselves not to look again in that direction.

I leaned against the door frame to my back porch in Maine as I started to read the essay; really, its existence astonished me, though I suppose I might have brushed the cat aside and sat in the rocking chair and taken a deep breath before I continued. I also might have sat in the rattan chair with the very comfortable cushion, or even on one of the benches pushed under the square picnic table, above which dangled a fuchsia plant that dropped perfectly formed but apparently useless flower bombs on its surface. Today was the Fourth of July, which reminded me of the president, and of his intention to have M1 tanks roll down the streets of DC, which wasn't a visual image that came easily to me.

Neither could I comprehend Gomer's essay, which ranged from unlikely to untrue, from fallacious to ridiculous. He wrote that he and I – the now-named Grover and I – had once been involved in a *folie à trois*, with our professor, who had pitted us against each other as a way of retaining our deepest affections. I was apparently 'asexual', and Gomer, *Grover*, had not yet 'come out'. Oh? I hadn't heard about that, and certainly hadn't suspected it when we'd had our long-ago lunch, too expensive for our budgets, at the sidewalk cafe.

What I remembered our having talked about, that day, was death. Now, that subject might logically be on our minds, but back then, we'd simply drifted into it because we'd both suffered losses. My brother had died at sixteen of a terrible cancer. Grover's beloved hound dog, Maggie May (this was years ago), had been killed by a taxi that jumped the curb in Boston, the day he'd gone to audition for the role of Rosencrantz in summer stock. The death of a dog, that way, was a very unlikely thing to happen. Also, Maria, the twin sister of Initials (our nickname for our professor, since he went exclusively by his initials, RB), had died of dehydration on her honeymoon, soon after the time we left school. Initials had contacted both of us. Dehydration! It was incomprehensible, as was the bizarre way her new husband had acted, needing to be bailed out of jail after a night of drinking, during which time he destroyed . . . was it store windows? He'd bashed in windows? Something. In any case, she was dead and he'd gone mad.

None of this, however, appeared in the essay – which I read rather frantically – and which focused on Gomer's, *Grover's*, inability, then, to understand that he was a pawn in our game, unwanted by either Initials or by me, yet necessary to what we both needed: an obstacle, a human obstacle, to our being together and being a conventional couple. Because, said he – and why not pull out all the stops? – in our triangle, any side that was struck excited the other side with the reverberation, and that, alone, had always been Initials's goal, as he was a closeted homosexual, with vast amounts of misplaced anger toward both women and men. Reading, I could easily understand why things had gotten to the point where everyone wanted their sexuality to be the first thing anyone knew about them now. But what, possibly, could have been the point of publishing something about our threesome – whatever it might have been – that had taken place in the Dark Ages? I paid little attention to how Gomer segued into #MeToo, so eager was I to see how the essay concluded. Its conclusion: 'I fell from my heights faster than Icarus to become an Uber driver.' This was the first sentence of the last paragraph? Was he being intentionally funny? The drivel continued, though I could barely continue reading: 'All day, I listen to other people's unsolicited stories and think how necessary it is to people that they take center stage, though the American experiment has ever been one of asserting one's individuality, even as we vanish into the crowd.'

It was *terrible*. Ghastly. Also, creepily, the sentence cadences appeared to have been deliberately constructed to echo the way I spoke, about which I'd taken a lot of kidding. What, possibly, could Gomer, *Grover*, intend? No one even knew who Initials and I were! I'd published one chapbook, thirty-some years before, in an edition of fifty numbered copies (I'd had an affair with the printer), and two short stories (three had been accepted, but only two were ever published) many years before that. I'd rarely thought of Initials, though I'd heard through the grapevine that he was in a nursing home – information so old, it was more likely he was dead.

I sent one of my long-ago classmates who'd for many years worked for the *San Francisco Chronicle* an email; he was right back to me, with information. He embodied links to the three best-rated nursing homes in the Washington, DC, area – and bingo! On the third call, it was clear, when I asked if Initials was there, that they knew the name, though I'd been right: he was dead. They didn't say that, but the strained silence gave me my answer.

Next, I called Grover, and was sent immediately to voicemail, where I had the restraint not to say my name, but, rather, 'I'm sure you know why I'm calling.' After that – phone hot in my hand – I called the only writer I knew, my friend Gigi, whose mother I'd nursed through her last illness. Gigi's mysteries were currently in development for Netflix. I'd reached her at a spa in Vermont, she told me. Is this legal? was my question for her. Can you use a real person's real name *and* their photograph, then say whatever you want about them? She gave me the answer I expected but also had a good idea: Call the editor and ask what the hell he or she thought they were doing. She asked me the name of the magazine twice. I think the second time she wrote it down. This was a terrible transgression, what they'd done, she said. It didn't seem possible, though in the age of Trump . . . She apologized for bringing up his name. 'Obviously, you could sue the writer, or the magazine, or both, but why would you want to get involved in that? Get something from them, instead.'

'What?' I asked.

'I don't know. Do Harry and David still have Fruit-of-the-Month Club?'

She apologized if it might seem that she hadn't been taking the situation seriously enough; I told her that even I couldn't take it seriously, but it seemed like such a violation of my privacy. It was so disconcerting. We hung up, promising to speak the next day.

I cold-called the magazine. I found the number inside the front cover. On the second ring, which did surprise me, a male voice answered. I asked to speak to the editor. 'You're in luck,' he said. 'If you'd wanted anybody else, I'd have to admit that the whole staff was either laid off, or they quit.' He said that he was putting out the magazine single-handedly. He'd been feeling sorry for himself because it was the Fourth of July.

I told him he published garbage. I summarized what I'd read in the essay, sounding none too coherent myself. I was shaking his flimsy little magazine in the air; that's why I couldn't find the title of the essay when he asked. I demanded to know whether he'd even tried to contact me, or Initials – obviously, not letting on that I knew Initials was dead. Asexual, I thought, indignantly. *Asexual!* The longer he remained silent, the angrier I became: He *could not do this; it was reprehensible, slanderous*; there'd be legal action; he was clearly incompetent. I threw the magazine to my feet.

'Jesus,' he said. 'Could we at least have coffee?'

What? Where did he think I was? Did he simply assume everyone was where *he* was, was that more of his stupidity, more of his head stuck in the sand? Who'd simply ask someone across the country to have coffee with them? He supposed I might be, Oh, at the cafe of *his* local bookstore? Taking a break from my job at the ski resort on the edge of town? At my boutique, hand-lettering labels for CBD oil?

'Well, where?' he asked. 'My phone's broken. It doesn't ID the caller.'

'New Hampshire,' I replied. 'I'm slightly more than an hour away from Boston,' I added, then wondered why I'd said that. (I'd also called it 'fucking Boston'.)

'Listen, I'm really upset,' he said. 'Really. I heard everything you said. We've just . . . I had no idea the writer used your real name. Anyone who writes for the magazine has to sign off on a work of fiction truly being a work of fiction, so he would have to have done that, though I realize that's not much consolation.'

'It's an essay, a lying *essay!*' I said.

'It was submitted as a short story,' he said, after a pause. 'Look at the table of contents.'

'I don't care what he called it! You – you, personally – ran a picture of us. What did you think it was? Just a random illustration the writer sent along? *Of me in my bathing suit?*'

He cleared his throat. 'Well, you know . . .' he began. He seemed surprised I didn't interrupt. He began again. 'You know, in, let's say, Sebald, there are photographs that are found photographs. You know what I'm saying? Just . . . found photographs.'

'*But you are talking to the person who is standing in the photograph you ran, which accompanies an essay that is about her life.*'

'Then I guess I'm up shit creek without a paddle,' he said. 'This'll be the last straw.' He either cleared his throat again or snorted. He said, 'There's no staff, as it is, like I said. Here I am, trying to pull the final issue together, but you know what? It's all just shit. You're right. I'd only be making a tombstone to deteriorate in tonight's rain like cheap motel soap.' He almost spat the last two words. Maybe he did spit. There was a hissing sound as he said 'soap'.

'Who is this guy?' the editor asked. His voice was low enough that he seemed to be whispering into my ear. I heard pages turning.

Actually, it was more like the sound of a page being ripped. He read aloud, sneeringly, like a schoolboy forced to recite: 'Grover Delaney lives in Williamsburg, Brooklyn, with his rescue dog, Plath, and his cat, Andrea Doria.'

I hadn't thought to look at his bio, but my God! Even the animals' names were a weird in-joke: Sylvia Plath wrote about the sinking of the ship, the *Andrea Doria*. Back in Initials's 'Intro to Poetry' class, we'd found it alarmingly chilling. But wait: maybe he didn't have a dog and a cat. Maybe that, too, was invented.

'Williamsburg, Brooklyn,' the editor said. 'I suppose if I was in New York, and a real magazine editor, the "Brooklyn" part would be implied. So what was going on here? It's some revenge thing, love gone wrong, or something?'

Though that didn't seem even a remote possibility, a strange thing came back to me as I heard myself, panting. I remembered that day at the lake, when the child had cut himself: Initials had sprung up and turned toward the outcropping of wet rocks, yet he'd almost instantly recoiled, nearly losing his footing, as the big woman reappeared, her expression one of pure rage. I'd seen it in the frightening flash of a second and turned away, a coward. And Gomer – he'd instantly grabbed my hand and squeezed. As Initials sat down, embarrassed that he'd lacked the courage to resist the woman, I'd seen Gomer's eyes connect with Initials's, though what of that, so what? It could also have been something I'd invented.

'The whole country's got other stuff on its mind right now,' the editor was saying. 'The Fourth of July. "God Bless America." My great-grandma's favorite singer in the world, Kate Smith, completely discredited. Trump's tanks rolling down the streets, rooms below statues cracking and being destroyed, the military flying overhead, migrants dying for lack of water, kids without food.'

I cupped my hand to my cheek, but he couldn't see that. He couldn't, that is, until he suggested we switch to FaceTime. Why not, I thought. Why not. I'd learned to use FaceTime when I'd subbed for my friend Evelyn as a hospice aide. So we set up our visual chat.

Soon, I found myself gazing up the long, white log of the editor's throat, into the darkness of his cavernous nostrils. My only thought was: *He's just a kid.*

And what must he have thought of me – the troublemaker, the difficult old lady, the person capable of ruining his last, optimistic gesture of producing one final magazine: a calling card, maybe, if another job was ever to be found in our Land of Losers.

'Why did you say "Stay bald" to me?' I asked.

'Say what?' he asked. He had bulging biceps. There was a tattoo on one, though all I could see below the cuff of his rolled-up shirt was the tail end of something: the coiled tail of some animal, maybe. 'Say again?' he said.

'When we were talking about the photograph. You told me to stay bald.'

'Sorry?' he said.

'When I told you that the photograph was of me. That I was the person you were looking at. You *said –*'

'Oh! *Sebald!* Sebald, sure. A really amazing writer. *The Rings of Saturn. Austerlitz.* Really, the guy was a genius. German. He found old photographs and dropped them into his text. Yeah, he died too young. The guy was a genius. Everybody thought he'd win the Nobel.'

Okay. I'd take the recommendation. I hoped to remember it, though I didn't have a pen. Of course, I could walk into the house and look for a pen.

'Imagine how surprised I was to open the magazine and see a picture of myself,' I said. 'It came yesterday. I might have carried it upstairs and not gotten to it for days, weeks. I might never have seen it. But I threw it on the kitchen island, with the rest of the mail, and today I opened it, and what did I see but that stupid essay, accompanied by a picture of me.'

'How old are you there?' he asked. He'd turned to that page.

'Seventeen. I started college early.'

'Managed to pay off your student loan, then, I guess?'

Books were stacked precariously behind him, I saw, as he shifted in the chair, giving me a different view of the room. It seemed small. A blind with broken slats hung at the only window I could see. A spiky plant in a pot sat below it.

'I didn't go into debt,' I said. 'My parents saved and sent me there to college. It was where my mother had dreamed of going.'

'*This college?*' he asked. He sounded even younger when he was surprised.

'Yes. That's how I came to subscribe to the magazine.'

His face moved so close to the camera, it became blurry before it wavered into focus, though for several seconds he had the nostrils of a horse. That was probably what brought my late father to mind, and his way of describing certain people as having 'a hangdog face'. My father had been misdiagnosed. He'd died of stomach cancer. Two years before, my mother had tumbled down the basement steps. She never regained consciousness. There was a baseball cap atop a pile of books beside the editor's computer, next to a plug-in keyboard and two coffee mugs, though I hadn't been looking at the hat, but rather remembering my parents.

'The magazine's come for over forty years,' I said. 'Imagine.'

'You must be our longest subscriber,' he said.

'Come to think of it, automatic renewals weren't usual back then, I don't think. Maybe my guardian angel saw to it that it kept coming.'

'Have you lived in the same place since you left here?' he asked.

I'd lived in two apartments and four different houses. The first house, my husband and I had lost when we'd declared bankruptcy. I was twice a widow at age sixty-four. 'Always in the same town, yes,' I replied.

'Wow. So I assume you like it there?'

'Live Free or Die.'

'State motto,' he said.

I had to admit, there didn't seem much left to talk about. I started to wonder how I could have let anyone see me wearing my baggy shirt, hair uncombed, glasses pushed to the top of my head. I said 'I published a story in your magazine once, but it was a few yea after I graduated, so that must have been, what? Over forty years ago.'

'I'll look it up,' he said. 'What's your last name?'

In fact, the story had been published under my maiden name, before I married Carlson, so it was good he'd asked. At least Gomer hadn't used my last name. I told the editor what my former name had been. I embarrassed myself by saying that my next story had come out in the *Sewanee Review*. I did think better of bragging about my poetry book, which had been published that same year. And that had been the end of that.

Apparently, I'd *said*, aloud, 'That was the end of that,' because the editor's follow-up question was, 'Haven't been writing up a storm since then, or haven't been lucky?', that slight tone of puckishness creeping into his voice.

'I became a nurse practitioner,' I said. What I'd really wanted to say, though, was that I didn't believe in so-called guardian angels, though in my line of work, there were times when it was easiest to just go with the flow. 'I enjoyed my work,' I said, 'though I understand that "enjoyed" is probably an odd word to choose. I recently retired. And I'm still a big reader.'

There was interference on the line. It wasn't static, though: behind him, the blind had fallen, toppling the plant, startling both of us. 'I'm sorry?' he said, trying to recover himself – by which he meant that he'd only heard the first part of my reply. But I liked what he'd said better the other way: I liked 'I'm sorry' better as a statement than as a question.

As I turned my head, I realized that the porch screen was torn, and that my beloved, docile cat was racing through the flap, making a merciless midair dive for a bird pecking below the suet ball.

I sprinted so fast I dropped the phone, the screen door slamming behind me, but it was too late: the mourning dove hadn't escaped.

'Hello? Hello?' he said, the anxiety obvious in his voice. 'HELLO?' he shouted. What might he be seeing? My porch roof, with the silver nailheads? My sloping lawn, at some odd angle? It was as if a spell had been broken. I heard him on the other end, but blood rushed to my head, and I also didn't hear. The cat, mouth clamped on its prize, had run under the climbing hydrangea. 'Hey, hello, hello, hello, hel-*lo*?' I heard, though it seemed to me that our story – at least, some story – had concluded. That I should wait a moment, without feeling any obligation to fill the void. Wait, then return to the porch, pick up the phone that lay silent, and sink into the rocking chair where I'd hoped to sit all along. ■

ICA Daily
Tuesday 26 May 2020

Einstürzende Neubauten

Sign up for ICA Daily at www.ica.art

Listen

Einstürzende Neubauten

Having tested positive for Covid-19 antibodies, I've temporarily moved my home office to Berlin. Last week the seminal German industrial group Einstürzende Neubauten released their new album *Alles in Allem* [All in All]. Timing is everything – right now is a perfect time to revisit the Neubauten's 40-year legacy, and through it read the (music) history of Berlin: The Garden (1996), Sehnsucht (1981), Interim Lovers (1993), Letztes Biest (1985), Alles in Allem (2020).
Stefan Kalmár

Join

Love Spells & Rituals for Another World

This virtual symposium curated by Lilly Markaki reflects on the powers of desire reinvigorated by black, feminist, and queer perspectives. It runs from 28 – 30 May and features contributions by Nat Raha, Chandra Frank, Mijke van der Drift, Keti Chukhrov and Antke Engel.
Sara Sassanelli

Watch

The Frankfurt School

Max Horkheimer and Theodor W. Adorno postulated on how the greatest danger to democracy would come from the mass-cultural apparatus of film, radio and television, and how they tend to operate to enforce conformity, quieten dissent and suppress thought. In this curious collage assembled from various TV clips, Horkheimer and Adorno address some of the founding principles of the Frankfurt School.
Nico Marzano

Read

Hao Jingfang: Folding Beijing

This incredible dystopian realist sci-fi novelette, recommended to me by climate change communicator Angela Chan, is a particularly striking read in these pandemic times. Angela runs wormworm.org and the London Chinese Sci-Fi Group @LondonChineseSF.
Rosalie Doubal

A Pandemic Trilogy

Drawing on the writings of Audre Lorde, Hannah Arendt, Naomi Klein and many more, in this collection of essays, writer and curator Cristina Morales shares her insights on what we can learn from the ways in which we are recovering from and resisting previous ways of being, living, and working. I'm particularly inspired by The Great Pause: A Decolonial Approach For Life Beyond Neoliberalism.
Nydia A. Swaby

How should we live? Density in post-pandemic cities

In this article for *Domus*, Richard Sennett writes on the implication of population density. What will cities, architecture and transport look like in our post-pandemic future?
Steven Cairns

Track of the Day

Arca: Time (20 May 2020)

Together we can do more!
Please consider supporting our work by subscribing to ICA Red Membership today.

ICA

CONTRIBUTORS

Ken Babstock is the author of five collections of poetry, most recently *On Malice*. His collection *Methodist Hatchet* won the 2012 Griffin Poetry Prize. *Swivelmount* will be published in North America by Coach House Books in 2020. He lives in Toronto with his son.

Kurt Beals is Associate Professor in the Department of Germanic Languages and Literatures at Washington University in St Louis.

Ann Beattie's books include the story collections *What Was Mine*, *The State We're In* and *The Accomplished Guest*. Her most recent novel is *A Wonderful Stroke of Luck*.

Viken Berberian is the author of the novels *The Cyclist* and *Das Kapital*, and the graphic novel *The Structure is Rotten, Comrade*, with illustrator Yann Kebbi.

Emma Cline is the author of *The Girls*. 'A/S/L' is taken from her story collection *Daddy*, forthcoming from Chatto & Windus in the UK and Random House in the US.

Teju Cole's recent books include the essay collection *Known and Strange Things* and the photobook *Fernweh*. He is a professor in the Department of English at Harvard University.

Joe Dunthorne is the author of three novels: *Submarine*, *Wild Abandon* and *The Adulterants*. A collection of his poems, *O Positive*, was published in 2019.

Jenny Erpenbeck is the author of *Go, Went, Gone* and *The End of Days*, which received the 2015 Independent Foreign Fiction Prize. Her collection of essays, *Not a Novel*, translated from the German by Kurt Beals, will be published by Granta Books.

Janine di Giovanni is a Senior Fellow at Yale University's Jackson Institute for Global Affairs. Her most recent book *The Morning They Came for Us: Dispatches from Syria* was translated into thirty languages. She is currently writing a book about Christians in the Middle East called *The Vanishing*, to be published in 2021.

Mark Haddon is the author of the story collection *The Pier Falls*, and four novels, including *The Curious Incident of the Dog in the Night-Time* and, most recently, *The Porpoise*.

Lisa Halliday has lived in Italy since 2011. Her first novel, *Asymmetry*, was published in twenty languages, and was a finalist for the 2018 National Book Critics Circle John Leonard Prize. She received a Whiting Award for Fiction in 2017.

Will Harris is the author of *RENDANG*, published by Granta Books in 2020. He was co-editor of the spring 2020 issue of the *Poetry Review*.

Colin Herd is a poet and lecturer at the University of Glasgow. His collections include *Too Ok*, *Glovebox*, *Click + Collect* and *You Name It*.

Michael Hofmann is a poet and German translator. His most recent collection of poems is *One Lark, One Horse*. He is a *Granta* contributing editor.

Joanna Kavenna is the author of various works of fiction and non-fiction including *The Ice Museum, Inglorious, The Birth of Love* and *A Field Guide to Reality*. She was named as one of *Granta*'s Best of Young British Novelists in 2013. Her latest novel is *Zed*.

Rachel Long is a poet and the founder of Octavia, a poetry collective for womxn of colour. Her debut poetry collection, *My Darling from the Lions*, is forthcoming from Picador in the UK.

Diana Matar is an artist working with photography, testimony and archive. She is the author of *Evidence* and the forthcoming *My America*. Her works have been exhibited or collected by Tate Modern, the National Museum of Singapore, the Victoria and Albert Museum and the Institut du Monde Arabe, Paris.

David Means is the author of five story collections including *Instructions for a Funeral*, and the novel *Hystopia*, which was longlisted for the 2016 Man Booker Prize.

China Miéville is the author of various works of fiction and non-fiction, and a founding editor of the journal *Salvage*.

Adam Nicolson writes memoir and non-fiction, including *Perch Hill, Sea Room, When God Spoke English* and *The Mighty Dead*. He is the winner of the Wainwright, Ondaatje, William Heinemann and Somerset Maugham prizes. He is a *Granta* contributing editor.

Jason Ockert is the author of *Wasp Box*, a novel, and two collections of short stories, *Rabbit Punches* and *Neighbors of Nothing*.

Sam Sax is a queer Jewish writer and educator. *Bury It* won the James Laughlin Award from the Academy of American Poets and he is the two-time Bay Area Grand Slam Champion. He has received the Ruth Lilly Fellowship from the Poetry Foundation and is currently a fellow at Stanford University.

Leanne Shapton is an author, artist and publisher. *Swimming Studies* won a 2012 National Book Critics Circle Award, and her most recent book is *Guestbook: Ghost Stories*. She is a *Granta* contributing editor, and painted the cover of this issue.

Wiktoria Wojciechowska is an artist working with photography, video, collage and installation. She was born in Lublin, Poland, in 1991 and currently lives between Paris and Lublin.